Football, Family, Gender and Identity

This book presents a cross-disciplinary examination of the lived experiences of girls and women football players using theoretical insights from sports studies, psychology, sociology and gender studies.

It examines the concept of 'the football self' – your own, personal football identity that encapsulates the importance of football to our everyday lives – and what that can tell us about the complex relationships between sport, family, gender and identity. The book draws on in-depth ethnographic research involving players and family members, and offers important new insights into the everyday experiences of those girls and women who play. It breaks new ground in focusing on the significant relationships between player and family with a particular focus on parenting through football. The book brings to the fore key debates around gender identity, barriers to participation, cultural gaps and discrimination. The author also brings a personal perspective to bear, drawing on experience gained over 20 years as a player, adding an extra critical layer to her important empirical research.

This is essential reading for all researchers and students with an interest in football, sport studies or issues around gender, inclusion or the family in sport, and fascinating reading for anybody generally curious about football.

Hanya Pielichaty is Associate Professor at the University of Lincoln, UK. Dr Pielichaty's research and teaching expertise relate to the sociology of sport and sports business management.

Critical Research in Football

Series Editors:
Pete Millward, Liverpool John Moores University, UK
Jamie Cleland, University of Southern Australia
Dan Parnell, University of Liverpool, UK
Stacey Pope, Durham University, UK
Paul Widdop, Manchester Metropolitan University, UK

The *Critical Research in Football* book series was launched in 2017 to showcase the inter- and multi-disciplinary breadth of debate relating to 'football'. The series defines 'football' as broader than association football, with research on rugby, Gaelic and gridiron codes also featured. Including monographs, edited collections, short books and textbooks, books in the series are written and/or edited by leading experts in the field whilst consciously also affording space to emerging voices in the area, and are designed to appeal to students, postgraduate students and scholars who are interested in the range of disciplines in which critical research in football connects. The series is published in association with the *Football Collective*, @FB_Collective.

Available in this series:

Football and Discrimination
Antisemitism and Beyond
Edited by Pavel Brunssen and Stefanie Schüler-Springorum

Football, Politics and Identity
James Carr, Daniel Parnell, Paul Widdop, Martin J. Power and Stephen R. Millar

Football, Family, Gender and Identity
The Football Self
Hanya Pielichaty

https://www.routledge.com/Critical-Research-in-Football/book-series/ CFSFC

Football, Family, Gender and Identity

The Football Self

Hanya Pielichaty

Routledge
Taylor & Francis Group

LONDON AND NEW YORK

First published 2021
by Routledge
2 Park Square, Milton Park, Abingdon, Oxon OX14 4RN

and by Routledge
605 Third Avenue, New York, NY 10017

Routledge is an imprint of the Taylor & Francis Group, an informa business

British Library Cataloguing-in-Publication Data
A catalogue record for this book is available from the British Library

Library of Congress Cataloging-in-Publication Data
A catalog record has been requested for this book

ISBN 13: 978-0-367-35235-6 (hbk)
ISBN 13: 978-1-03-204196-4 (pbk)

Typeset in Times New Roman
by codeMantra

This book is dedicated to my wonderful family: Mum, Dad, Joe, Gavin, Benji and Ada as well as the many friends I have made through football.

Contents

Figures

1 Introducing me and football

I was the first girl in the history of my primary school to play on the boys' football team. This had no significance to me at the time but it did create some interesting social situations. One of which took place at an awards ceremony following a tournament victory. My team and I were stood in a row waiting patiently for a man to put medals around our necks to symbolise our achievement. After each medal placement the man shook a player's hand before moving on to the next recipient. It was finally my turn; I proudly waited for my medal and handshake, even positioning my right hand out in front of me ready. But what followed wasn't a handshake at all... My parents described the next move to me (years later) as an almost falling backwards; I prefer to think of it as a 'Neo style' hyper-extension of the back, dodging bullets, akin to The Matrix film. It wasn't bullets that came towards me though, but rather the *medal man* had attempted to kiss me on the cheek! My response to which was to fling my face and body out of the way in a desperate scuttle to evacuate the area to much amusement from the parent spectators. As a nine year old footballer, the last thing you want is a kiss on the cheek! Where was my handshake?

My childhood bedroom walls were covered with centre-piece programme pull-outs of Andy Booth and Ronnie Jepson rather than more typical tributes to *Take That* and the *Spice Girls*. Growing up in the 90s in the English East Midlands, with a strange sounding last name, and a love for Huddersfield Town and all things football was not the classic formula for British girlhood.

Around the age of nine I seemed to do nothing but kick a ball about. I didn't think much of being the first ever girl to be selected for the *boys'* football team at primary school: I just wanted to play.

The relationship between school and football is extremely important (see Emmanuel, 2017; Clark and Paechter, 2007; Swain, 2000). My love for football continued into my later school years. The step up to secondary school is significant in terms of child development and sustaining participation in sport. In general, from late childhood, girls' and boys' opportunities to participate in mixed sports lessons become limited. There are schools in the UK that continue to segregate PE lessons on the basis of gender, even though they are not required to do so, a potential legacy from the Victorian era (Lawson, 2013). As Stirling and Schulz comment, 'whatever strides are gained become lost as soon as the girls commence secondary school, due to the absence of football from the curriculum' (Stirling and Schulz, 2011, 53). Only 47% of schools within the Union of European Football Associations (UEFA) member associations have football on the curriculum for girls (FIFA, 2014).

The Football Association's (FA) 2020–2024 strategy for girls' and women's football seeks to directly address this and create opportunities for all girls to access football (FA, 2020). My experiences of secondary school football were all positive but looking back there were structural issues to overcome. I had to set up the first ever girls' football team at secondary school (assisted by a female French teacher) because at that time the FA no longer permitted girls over the age of 11 to play with boys. Sixty-three per cent of the Fédération Internationale de Football Association (FIFA) member associations now offer mixed football (FIFA, 2019). Arguably, this FA ruling stunted the progress of girls' and women's football in England, having negative ramifications for decades to come.

The reason my footballing experience at school was so positive and impactful was because of my inspirational Physical Education (PE) teacher: Mr Curry (now Dr Curry). Mr Curry found ways to encourage my football participation and gave me confidence to play. We would talk endlessly about football, and on one occasion he gave me a signed Huddersfield Town poster, a gift from Kevin Gray, a Huddersfield Town defender and former pupil of Mr Curry. I remember during my time in 6th Form Mr Curry took a sabbatical; he later returned with his PhD thesis (concerning the origins of football) for me to read, labelled 'homework' – I was pleased to return the favour to him 16 years later with my own. I am still in contact with Dr Curry now, we exchange emails about academia and he even delivered a guest lecture to some of my first years not so long ago. The impact a teacher has on a child's life is fundamental to their future growth and potential; teachers maintain privileged positions.

Figure 1.1 Lincoln City Ladies FC Reserves circa 2000.

During my school years I played district- and county-level football and for Lincoln City Ladies FC Reserves. Playing for Lincoln was my first experience of 'serious' football, and I am still friends with many of the players today. The coaching team at Lincoln was excellent and did everything possible to progress me as a player and to develop the game locally. My entry into the first team at Lincoln, however, coincided with my departure for university so I waved goodbye to the city of Lincoln (for the time being) (Figure 1.1).

I went to the University of Warwick to study Psychology and Philosophy. Whilst there, I scored over 90 goals; a personal highlight was scoring three hat tricks in one game. Immediately after Warwick I went to study my Master's degree at the University of Sheffield in Sport and Recreation Management. At the end of my one season with the Sheffield university team I was awarded *Players' Player* and *Player of the Year* awards.

After university I played for two seasons with West Bromwich Albion (WBA) Women FC (mostly Reserves), an amazing experience

I will never forget. I moved to the West Midlands for work, and football provided me with a route into friendship and a new community. Dave Smith, the Assistant Coach at WBA, had a profound impact on me personally and my playing ability. He believed in me as a player and person; his confidence gave me confidence. He was academically minded, so we would spend time discussing pedagogy and analysing football, and he compared football to the Samba, meaning each move had rhythm and a sequence to it. I desperately wanted to play well at WBA but became so disheartened when my mind prevented me from being 'free' to enjoy the game. Dave knew that my analytical side was a challenge, and so he offered to coach me for an extra hour every Thursday evening. So my two-hour training session became three hours whereby Dave would coach me through shooting drills away from the other players. I was very grateful for his help at the time but even more so now, realising that Dave had decided to spend additional time, after work to volunteer and help me. The people serving grassroots football really are phenomenal. The extra training worked, and I gained in confidence and also became noticed more by the first team management. At this point, however, my work contract was nearly up and I wanted to move back 'home'. When I returned to the East Midlands I briefly dabbled with retirement but then played for two more seasons with Nettleham Ladies before properly retiring during the 2015/2016 season. By the time I had stopped playing football I had clocked up over two decades of consistent and dedicated participation, paying to play a sport I loved.

But why is any of this important? Well, it's important because football books do not normally platform girls' and women's voices, and certainly not the voices of *everyday* players: the ones that battle on undulating pitches and where the subs have to run the line. And also, my voice as a female author, academic and former footballer is here pulling together my own personal stories alongside those of the players that will feature in this book. This is an activist book, framed by feminism and understood through a lens of 'gender justice' (Watson and Scraton, 2017; Pielichaty, 2021a, 2021b), allowing me to combat the 'silencing of the female ethnographer in sport research' (Richards, 2015, 393) which can and does occur. This leads me to the book's purpose: to examine gender, identity and family relationships within girls' and women's football. The concept of the 'football self' is important to this book and can be understood as the meaning football has to those that play, the position it takes within their lives. This book is personal, and as a departure from other academic texts I will be using my own standpoint epistemology (Sprague, 2016) and football experiences to position and understand the historical and contemporary landscape of girls' and women's football in England.

There has been a significant increase in participation rates in women's football (Woodward, 2017), and FIFA (2018, 10) aspires to 'double the number of female players to 60 million by 2026'. In 2018 the FA ensured all 11 teams within the Women's Super League (WSL) were full-time and professional in status and had an academy feeder club. An influx of sponsorship also helped to fuel the professional status of women's football, an example being VISA partnering with the Union of European Football Associations on a seven-year deal (UEFA, 2018). Furthermore, England finished fourth in the FIFA Women's World Cup in 2019 and it has been agreed that the 2023 Women's World Cup tournament will expand to accommodate 32 teams (FIFA, 2020).

Despite these positive shifts and numerical changes it is more difficult to see whether there has been a cultural change in society's view towards girls and women in and around football (see Pielichaty, 2020; Woodhouse et al., 2019). Dunn and Welford (2015) explain that women's football is isolated from the normative construction of what football 'is' to the masses, namely a sport for men to play and enjoy. The first report on women footballers' working conditions stated that 50% of 'professional' players globally do not get paid to play the game, with the majority negotiating their participation alongside study or another job (FIFPro, 2017). FIFA (2018, 4) themselves understand that there is still much more work to be done reporting that 'the game is both in rude health and in need of fundamental change'. Furthermore, the Covid-19 pandemic is anticipated to significantly impact elite women's football with the cancellation of the 2919/2020 WSL season and concerns over the uncertainty of the women's game (Clarkson et al., 2020). Financial assistance of over one million pounds has been granted by the Premier League to help the WSL and the Women's Championship to recover from the pandemic (Daniels, 2020).

It seems women's football is enduring a time of concomitant narratives: one of progress and one of cultural stagnation (see Woodward, 2017). This highlights another important purpose of this book, and that is to provide a critical and contemporary view of girls' and women's football from the perspective of those who play amidst this contradictory backdrop. An increase in participation numbers does not directly correlate to a change in social attitudes towards girls' and women's appropriateness to football. This examination will continue in Chapter 2 in much more depth and considers global perspectives.

The premise of this book is to provide you, the reader, with an insight into how girls and women experience football participation alongside other facets of their lives. Stone (2007, 170) explained 'it is in the everyday life that football culture is primarily perpetuated, expressed and experienced', and it is the *everyday* aspect that will be of importance to this book. The heart of this text is about a love for football and the meaning that the sport has to those who play. As such, the chapters are structured in a way to encourage story-building, each chapter feeding in and out of the next in an attempt to understand the importance and placement of football within the lives of the players and their families. Even though the chapters have been organised into discrete areas, this does not mean to reflect an isolation and/or clean separation of the topics discussed. As always, the themes of gender and identity are complex, nuanced and murky, blurring in and out of each other like ink on blotting paper.

As already highlighted the following chapter will provide an in-depth and critical look at the current state of girls' and women's football from across the globe. Furthermore, previous football studies and their methodological approaches will be considered in order to understand the ways girls' and women's experiences have been viewed and explored before. Chapter 3 will delve into the notion of the 'football self', an original concept presented in my earlier empirical work which depicts the meaning of football to a particular player (see Pielichaty, 2019). The football self in connection with identity will be examined and underpinned by socio-psychological approaches to identity. The Football Self Continuum also outlined in previous work (Pielichaty, 2019) will be presented as a heuristic device to understand the fluidity and mobility of identities through participation. It is important to first have discussed identities per se before moving onto gender as placed in Chapter 4. The outdated but maintained gender boundaries connecting to girlhood and football participation will be explored through the voices of players themselves. The notion of 'authenticity' and beauty will also be examined whereby players have preconceived ideas surrounding the 'right' way to perform 'player'.

Chapter 5 is the first of two family-focused chapters in which the relationships between footballer and family are closely investigated. First, the notion of the 'football family' will be discussed as well as the importance of the football-playing daughter/sister to the family unit. Themes of family identity, bonding and pressure will formulate this chapter to present an understanding of the way football transcends into home life. Chapters 6 and 7 progress this further and provide an in-depth view of the everyday lives of football parents and their daughters. Chapter 6 examines the way parents act as 'conspicuous' or 'inconspicuous' football parents, and Chapter 7 looks at the gendered aspect of football parenting. It must be noted that sibling relationships will not be a key feature of this book but further reading is available in Pielichaty (2021a). The final chapter of this book will focus on the future of girls' and women's football, going beyond the football self to understand how players will progress at individual and societal levels. A consideration of the implications this text has to policy and praxis will be outlined, and a strategy for gender justice in girls' and women's football will be presented.

Weaving between the data and the me

This book is a culmination of several years' academic work, drawing upon my PhD research and subsequent body of work[1, 2] to supplement my theoretical viewpoint. Alongside this my own experiences gained from playing football for over 20 years will be utilised; this will be achieved by layering personal accounts of participation alongside academic findings. As mentioned already I would never consider myself to have been an elite player, and therefore, my position is one of an everyday, passionate player (now former player) which is important in terms of how I portray voice within this book.

Due to the nature of this examination it was extremely important to implement a research design and methodology which were consistent with the outlook and experiences of the researcher. Feminism, therefore, sits at the core of this book but there is no one way of being a feminist or conducting feminist research. Feminism was born out of the subordination of women and is generally epitomised by arguments about nature, difference, femininity, weakness and power. There are many differing forms of feminism(s) but ultimately they all share one thing in common, the belief that women are valuable (Crawford, 2006).

Extending this further, it is critical feminism that underpins this book's philosophy and the way I conduct my research. Critical feminism focuses on the socio-historical discriminatory practices and structures that impact contemporary understandings of inequality. Critical feminism provides the scope for my own researcher involvement and allows me to adopt both an *involved* and a *critical* position (see Ray and Fine, 1999). It provides an effective way into the study of football, to address the ingrained gender relations in football culture. Not only does this book seek to understand the meaning of football to the girls and women who play but also how these players negotiate and manage barriers to participation. It is important that the seemingly crystallised 'facts' (Lincoln and Guba, 2000) about women's capabilities are challenged by a re-search design that facilitates collaboration and freedom of expres-sion and which is socially transformative. This is also the basis in which a 'gender justice' lens can be adopted to provide insight into the study's findings in connection with social activism and change, as reported in the final chapter.

Collaborating with footballers and their families

The study in which this book is based utilises data that were un-dertaken across three types of research site: a football academy, a secondary school and family homes. Over 120 players and family members took part over the season-long study through observa-tions, focus groups and individual and family interviews. All three types of site represent influential social spaces which impact upon both football experiences and gender. The academy was a county-wide organised football club which accommodated talented girls across five age categories: under nines (U9s), under 11s (U11s), under 13s (U13s), under 15s (U15s) and under 17s (U17s). Players attended a trial in the summertime prior to the start of the season to assess their ability levels ahead of being invited to join the academy. The girls and young women who played for the academy were provided with team kit, transport for matches and the opportunity to play against other competing academy sites across England. The players had to pay a fee to join the academy, which covered training costs, pitch hire, transport, kit and other related expenditure. Over 90 players and parents (including one grandparent) took part in the research at the academy, whether through observations and/or interviews.

The secondary school which took part in the research was a mixed academy school. Both observational research and focus group conversations were conducted with girls from the joint year seven and eight football team (U13s) and the year ten football team (U15s) between the months of September and April. Focus groups were chosen to ensure the girls felt comfortable amongst close peers and due to the practicalities of engaging with more players within the constraints of a school day; interactive activities were used to make the focus group conversations more effective and constructive. Observations complemented the focus group approach as they allowed for fluid research notes to be taken during the 'natural' football setting.

In total 18 girls and young women took part at this research site, ten from the younger age group and eight from the U15s team. Girls were selected via purposive sampling by their PE teacher; in order to be eligible, players had to be part of one of the two school football teams. Furthermore, two girls in the U13s team and three girls in the U15s team also played for local clubs outside of school. I actively participated in the girls' football practices, and after-school matches in the autumn term to build up a rapport with them before conducting the focus group conversations in the spring term.

The final type of site was that of the family home. Conversational interviews with family members and/or football-playing daughters were mainly conducted in their family homes. In total, five families' lives were explored (13 people in total); in one case, only the footballer was interviewed but this was still categorised as the 'family' aspect of the research because of the content of the discussion. Each family centred on a football-playing daughter(s) who was either still playing or had retired from the game. All the players involved across the family site had played or still played football at club standard, which ranged from mid-tier women's football through to international level. In terms of reporting players' voices in this book, player ages will be stated if part of the academy or school team but adult players will simply be reported by name. All players have been given pseudonyms.

Utilising critical ethnography

Critical ethnography featured across both the academy site and the secondary school venue. Ethnography has been crucial in the development of childhood studies as an approach which allows children to actively shape their own social circles (James, 2007). Critical ethnography is fully accepting of the impossibility of the researcher's neutrality; it is also dedicated to bringing social issues to the forefront. It can thus be thought of as 'non-neutral', 'advocates against inequities and domination of particular groups' and seeks to 'identify and celebrate research bias' (Skinner, Edwards and Corbett, 2015, 163). Fitzpatrick and May (2016) advocate the adoption of critical ethnographies because they understand the importance of research context and particularly here the socio-historical one as significant to girls' and women's football.

At the academy I took on the role of volunteer coach for the season. This role spanned all five age categories which enabled me to move freely between group practices and helped me to build up a rapport with all players and coaches across the centre. The role included attendance at Monday evening training sessions throughout the football season. Anderson (2009, 13) states that 'my desire to be comfortable in my informants' social worlds enabled me to collect much of the "sensitive" data I show'. This is an important point; it demonstrates that the researcher must feel relatively at ease in the social sphere they occupy, so as to build up natural and trusting relationships. This was the case for me whereby I utilised the volunteer coach role effectively to access the routine experiences of the players and their families. Tedlock (2000, 455) describes ethnographers as 'cross-dressers', taken to mean that the outside researcher slowly learns about the insider's lives through the wearing of insider clothes and the acquisition of their language and behavioural norms. The academy provided coaching kit which assisted me to become a part of the football setting. I never felt like a 'cross-dresser', however; the football uniform, football colloquialisms and connected behaviours were familiar, comfortable and even nostalgic to me.

As a volunteer coach and an adult I automatically took on a position of power over the young football players; the coaches were there to teach and guide the players in a way which indicated authority. My role though was more informal, with less responsibility, which allowed me to establish rapport with the players and parents over the period. As I was not assigned to any one age group, the parents did not associate me with team selection for match days or key tactical decision-making and therefore felt comfortable to talk to me about their experiences. In a sense, I was able to operate within a fluid, liminal space, negotiating roles of player, coach and spectator. Due to my unique insider/outsider position, I believe the data collected to be rich, detailed and insightful.

I found flexibility and freedom in joining in with the players. Having no official coaching responsibility, I was able to move constantly from side to side along an observation continuum. The observation continuum describes involvement from pure observer to pure participant and all transitions in between (Pitney and Parker, 2009). The notion of participant observer can be described as oxymoronic (Tedlock, 2000) due to the differing objectives the role of participant and observer involves for the researcher. The continuum analogy is therefore deemed a more appropriate description to demonstrate the researcher's ethnographic involvement. This continuum in my experience related directly to the age group of the players I interacted with. For example, with the older age group, I aligned more heavily towards an observer role because the coaching sessions were serious, exacting and involved high-tempo and -quality performance-related drills. With the youngest age group, I was closer to the participant descriptor due to the informal nature of the sessions and the high levels of enjoyment involved. In each training session, I moved fluidly across the observer (outsider) and participant (insider) scale, to maintain appropriate levels of both researcher and volunteer coach professionalism.

I also implemented a critical ethnographic approach with the secondary school footballers. I was invited to attend the girls' after-school football sessions and matches in the capacity of volunteer coach. All pupils were aware that I was conducting a study about girls' football and were invited to participate. Six weeks of observations were made; this covered three fixtures and three practice sessions. My involvement varied dramatically from week to week and drifted constantly back and forth across the observer-participant continuum. Being involved in this manner across these two sites meant that I could connect with the players which helped me to understand their social worlds.

Reflections of the self

The extensive study in which this book is based draws together experiences of footballers and their families over an extended period. In order to reframe these experiences and develop their richness further I now seek to position my own stories and experiences of football participation alongside these players. The self-ethnographic aspect of this text, therefore, draws upon my memories and old photos and mementos to provide a structural and temporal framework for the 'story' being told (Armour and Chen, 2012).

A lot has been written academically about the role of personal experiences and reflections within the research field, and due to this many terms and phrases are often associated with this approach. According to Jones, Adam and Ellis (2013, 22) a commonality of all autoethnographies 'is the use of personal experience to examine and/or critique cultural experience'. Different approaches to autoethnographies have been used to provide a space for voice, change and political activism, such as Cox et al.'s (2017) examination of 'Law Four', restricting the wearing of headscarves in football. Autoethnography as a legitimate methodology has been advocated by academics who prioritise the importance of author subjectivity to access meaning (Allen-Collinson and Hockey, 2005) and offer 'fresh and innovative variation' (Allen-Collinson, 2016, 282).

In their examination of female fandom, Hoeber and Kerwin (2013, 330) utilised the term self-ethnography rather than autoethnography as they did not believe their work to be drawing on 'intensely personal' experiences as traditional to autoethnography. This is consistent with my own position in this book, and therefore, the approach of historical self-ethnography will be taken. I will be reflecting on experiences from my own football participation across a 20-year period which I will position alongside empirical data. The purpose of this approach is to frame the work both personally and academically but to also add an additional *texture* and historical perspective to the book.

The main way I will embed my own voice into this book will be through storytelling and the presentation of *memory snippets* which have resonance to my own participation and have shaped my development as a player, person and academic. Smith and Weed (2007, 256) explain that 'storytelling relations are a fundamental condition for how narratives generate and come to have meaning for people' (Smith and Weed, 2007, 256). It is thought that 'reflective techniques enable significant sport experiences to be remembered, problematised and written in narrative form' (Fleming and Fullagar, 2007, 240), and this is the basis for the current book. Reflections will platform and enrich empirical data to provide a holistic and personal account of gender, football and family relationships.

Conclusion

So there you have it; this is a football book, written by a former footballer about the meaning of football. The importance here, however, is how this meaning formulates and mediates within the world of girls' and women's football, an environment that lacks funding, resources and often cultural acceptance. How do these extraneous variables influence the meaning of football to the girls and women who play? This book seeks to address this further and to build upon previous work on football identities (Pielichaty, 2019) and performative pleasures (Pielichaty, 2020). Fundamentally I hope that you as a reader enjoy engaging with this book: this being my priority. If you are an undergraduate or postgraduate student, then I hope this book helps you to understand more about the girls' and women's football sphere and to encourage you to think critically about why and how these experiences came to be. If you are a fellow academic, I hope you find this read engaging and useful for your own teaching and research. Finally, if you are reading this for pleasure, thank you, and I hope you enjoy learning more about the game of football, shared by all people, but not necessarily held to account by the same cultural rules.

Notes

1 This book is derived in part from an article published in *Qualitative Journal of Sport, Exercise and Health* published online on 26.11.18 copyright Taylor & Francis, available online: https://www.tandfonline. com/doi/abs/10.1080/2159676X.2018.1549094?journalCode=rqrs21.
2 This book is also derived in part from the following article: Pielichaty, H, Pleasure and the Sanctuary Paradox: Experiences of Girls and Women Playing Soccer, International Review for the Sociology of Sport (55/6) pp. 788–806. Copyright © [2020] (Sage). doi:10.1177/1012690219857023.

References

Allen-Collinson, J. (2016) Autoethnography as the engagement of self/ other, self/culture, self/politics, selves/futures. In: Jones, S.H., Adam, T.E. and Ellis, C. (eds.) *Handbook of autoethnography*, 2nd edition. Oxon: Routledge, 281–299.

Allen-Collinson, J. and Hockey, J. (2005) Autoethnography: self-indulgent or rigorous methodology? In: McNamee, M. (ed.) *Philosophy and the sciences of exercise, health and sport: critical perspectives on research methods*. Oxon: Routledge, 177–191.

Anderson, E. (2009) *Inclusive masculinity: the changing nature of masculinities*. London: Routledge.

Armour, K. and Chen, H. (2012) Narrative research methods: where the art of storytelling meets the science of research. In: Armour, K. and Macdonald, D. (eds.) *Research methods in physical education and youth sport*. Oxon: Routledge, 237–249.

Clark, S. and Paechter, C. (2007) 'Why can't girls play football?' Gender dynamics and the playground." *Sport, Education and Society*, 12(3), 261–276.

Clarkson, B.G., Culvin, A. Pope, S. and Parry, K.D. (2020) Covid-19: reflections on threat and uncertainty for the future of elite women's football in England. *Managing Sport and Leisure*. doi:10.1080/23750472.202 0.1766377

Cox, M., Dickson, G. and Cox, B. (2017) Lifting the veil on allowing head-scarves in football: a co-constructed and analytical autoethnography. *Sport Management Review*, 20(5), 522–534.

Crawford, M. (2006) *Transformations: women, gender and psychology.* New York: McGraw-Hill.

Daniels, T. (2020) Women's football receives £1m boost from the Premier League. *Insider Sport.* Available from: https://insidersport.com/2020/07/01/womens-football-receives-1m-boost-from-the-premier-league/ [Accessed 1 July 2020].

Dunn, C. and Welford, J. (2015) *Football and the FA women's super league: structure, governance and impact.* London: Palgrave.

Emmanuel, M. (2017) 'Girls don't play soccer': children policing gender on the playground in a township primary school in South Africa. *Gender and Education*, 29(4), 476–494.

FA (2020) Inspiring positive change: the FA's strategy for women's and girls' football: 2020–2024. Available from: https://thefabrochures.co.uk/19268_WOMENS_GIRLS_FOOTBALL_STRATEGY_2020-24/index.html [Accessed 22 October 2020].

FIFA (2014) *Women's football survey.* Available form: https://resources.fifa.com/image/upload/fifa-women-s-football-survey-2522649.pdf?cloudid=emtgxvp0ibnebltlvi3b [Accessed 11 June 2019].

FIFA (2018) *Women's football strategy.* Available from: https://resources.fifa.com/image/upload/women-s-football-strategy.pdf?cloudid=z7w21ghir8jb9tguvbcq [Accessed 10 June 2020].

FIFA (2019) *Women's football member associations survey report 2019.* Available from: https://img.fifa.com/image/upload/nq3ensohyxpuxovcovj0.pdf [Accessed 8 July 2020].

FIFA (2020) *Making football truly global: the vision 2020–2023.* Zurich: FIFA.

FIFPro (2017) *2017 FIFPro global employment report: working conditions in professional women's football.* Available from: https://fifpro.org/attachments/article/6986/2017%20FIFPro%20Women%20Football%20Global%20Employment%20Report-Final.pdf [Accessed 15 May 2019].

Fitzpatrick, K. and May, S. (2016) Doing critical educational ethnography with Bourdieu. In: Murphy, M. and Costa, C. (eds.) *Theory as method in research: on Bourdieu, social theory and education.* Oxon: Routledge, 101–114.

Fleming, C. and Fullagar, S. (2007) Reflexive methodologies: an autoethnography of the gendered performance of sport/management graduate student research. *Annals of Leisure Research*, 10(3–4), 238–256.

Hoeber, L. and Kerwin, S. (2013) Exploring the experiences of female sport fans: a collaborative self-ethnography. *Sport Management Review*, 16(3), 326–336.

James, A. (2007) Ethnography in the study of children and childhood. In: Atkinson, P., Coffey, A., Delamont, S., Lofland, J. and Lofland, L. (eds.) *Handbook of ethnography.* London: Sage Publications, 246–257.

Jones, S.H., Adam, T.E. and Ellis, C. (2013) *Handbook of autoethnography.* Oxon: Routledge.

Lawson, S. (2013) School sports: ingraining the subtle art of segregation. *The Telegraph,* 22 December. Available from: http://www.telegraph. co.uk/education/educationopinion/10527651/School-sports-ingraining-the-subtle-art-of-segregation.html [Accessed 27 March 2017].

Lincoln, Y.S. and Guba, E.G. (2000) Paradigmatic controversies, contradictions, and emerging influences. In: Denzin, N. and Lincoln, Y. (eds.) *Handbook of qualitative research,* 2nd edition. London: Sage Publications, 163–188.

Pielichaty, H. (2019) Identity salience and the football self: a critical ethnographic study of women and girls in football. *Qualitative Research in Sport, Exercise and Health,* 11(4), 527–542.

Pielichaty, H. (2020) Pleasure and the Sanctuary Paradox: experiences of girls and women playing soccer. *International Review for the Sociology of Sport,* 55(6), 788–806.

Pielichaty, H. (2021a) Negotiating sibling relationships in girls' and women's football. In: Trussell, D. and Jeanes, R. (eds.) *Families, sport, leisure, and social justice.* London: Routledge.

Pielichaty, H. (2021b) Embedding gender justice in higher education: an example from sports business management. *IMPact,* 4(1), 1–8.

Pitney, W.A. and Parker, J. (2009) *Qualitative research in physical activity and the health professions.* Champaign: Human Kinetics.

Ray, R.E. and Fine, M. (1999) Researching to transgress: the need for critical feminism in gerontology. *Journal of Women and Aging,* 11(2/3), 171–184.

Richards, J. (2015) 'Which player do you fancy then?' Locating the female ethnographer in the field of sociology of sport. *Soccer and Society,* 16(2/3), 393–404.

Skinner, J., Edwards, A. and Corbett, B. (2015) *Research methods for sport management.* London: Routledge.

Smith, B. and Weed, M. (2007) The potential of narrative research in sports tourism. *Journal of Sport and Tourism,* 12(3–4), 249–269.

Sprague, J. (2016) *Feminist methodologies for critical researchers: bridging differences,* 2nd edition. Maryland: Rowman and Littlefield.

Stirling, L. and Schulz, J. (2011) Women's football: still in the hands of men. *Sport Management International Journal,* 7(2), 53–78.

Stone, C. (2007) The role of football in everyday life. *Soccer and Society,* 8(2/3), 169–184.

Swain, J. (2000) 'The money's good, the fame's good, the girls' are good': the role of playground football in the construction of young boys' masculinity in junior school. *British Journal of Sociology of Sport,* 21(1), 95–109.

Tedlock, B. (2000) Ethnography and ethnographic representation. In: Denzin, N. and Lincoln, Y. (eds.) *Handbook of qualitative research,* 2nd edition. London: Sage Publications, 455–486.

UEFA (2018) Visa signs ground-breaking seven-year women's football deal with UEFA. Available from: https://www.uefa.com/insideuefa/about-uefa/administration/marketing/news/newsid=2586330.html [Accessed 15 May 2019].

Watson, B. and Scraton, S. (2017) Gender justice and leisure sport feminisms. In Long, J. Fletcher, T. and Watson, B. (eds.) *Sport, leisure and social justice*. London: Routledge, 43–57.

Woodhouse, D., Fielding-Lloyd, B. and Sequerra, R. (2019) Big brother's little sister: the ideological construction of women's super league. *Sport in Society*, 22(12), 2006–2023.

Woodward, K. (2017) Women's time? Time and temporality in women's football. *Sport in Society*, 20(5–6), 689–700.

2 The girls' and women's footballscape

The landscape of girls' and women's football appears to be experiencing very fast-paced change. The FIFA Women's World Cup in 2019 'felt' different with a reported audience reach of over one billion globally (FIFA, 2019a) and contributed (directly and indirectly) 284 million Euros to France's economy (FIFA, 2020). The tournament games surpassed previous World Cups in terms of quality, technical ability, fitness and speed, which perhaps reflects the injection of funding and the increased professionalisation of some leagues across the world. This popularity fed into the start of the domestic season in England with 31,213 people attending the Manchester derby at the Etihad Stadium (Morgan, 2019a). There was also a reported increase range of 31%–35% in participation rates across several age bandings, with 460,000 more women (aged 25+) playing football after the tournament (Sport England, 2020).

There seems to be a real appetite for women's football within the UK and further afield which is demonstrated by increased media coverage, viewership and also commercial intrigue. Barclays now sponsor the Women's Super League (WSL) in a deal worth over £10 million (Wrack, 2019a) and the Football Association (FA) also launched the FA Player for 2019/2020 which will cover all of the WSL live games for the first time (McCaskill, 2019). On the European stage, VISA signed a seven-year deal with Union of European Football Associations (UEFA) to sponsor the women's game (Wrack, 2018) and Nike became UEFA's official match ball supplier for competitions as well as partnering them for the Together #WePlayStrong campaign (UEFA, 2019a). Since the Women's World Cup in 2019 it is thought that sponsors and brands are exploring how to capitalise on this significant time (Lyons, 2019). FIFA's (2020) *Vision for Making Football Truly Global* reports the potential for commercial investment:

The game has risen in both participation and interest, thus laying the foundation for the generation of higher commercial returns for the long-term benefit of the whole football movement.

(FIFA, 2020, 14)

Away from the big stage, the participation numbers for girls' and women's football continue to increase both domestically and globally (see Table 2.1).

Table 2.1 Participation Numbers of Girls and Women Footballers across the Globe

Location	Source	Statistics
Worldwide	FIFA (2014)	30,145,700 female players worldwide 4,801,360 total registered female players (senior and youth)
	FIFA (2019b)	13.36 million girls and women playing organised football 3.12 million registered youth players (U18) 945,068 registered adult players
Europe	FIFA (2014)	6,145,100 total female players 2,095,803 total female registered players
	UEFA (2016)	1,270,481 registered female players* 1,396 professional players
	UEFA (2017)	1,365,524 registered female players* 1790 professional players
	UEFA (2019b)	827,000 registered youth players (U18)
England	FIFA (2017)	2.05 million senior players (16+ years) 2.9 million youth players
	FIFA (2019b)	120,557 female players playing organised football 43,934 registered adult players 76,625 registered youth players (U18)
	FA (2020a)	3.4 million women and girls playing football 9,251 affiliated teams*
	FA (2020b)	2 million women (16+) and 1 million girls playing football 12,640 registered teams

* It is not clear from the source whether this means senior and/or youth players/teams

Table 2.1 reports upon several sources which seek to collate and disseminate participation numbers surrounding girls' and women's football; however, discrepancies are prevalent here. For example, it is difficult to make reliable comparisons due to the difference in the way the information is reported and who reports it, such as whether players are registered, playing 'organised' football and at what point age distinctions are made. Even the FA (2020c, 48) admits that there is 'Inconsistent data capture across the game' in relation to the *football for all* baseline measures. This aside, the participation picture remains positive, with growing numbers enjoying the game of football. As described on UEFA's (2019b) website:

> From humble and hopeful beginnings, and thanks to the unstinting work of UEFA, its national associations, dedicated officials and administrators and countless supporters and volunteers, the women's game has blossomed in spectacular style to become a football attraction in its own right – and the work goes on daily to promote and nurture women's football and attract more girls and women to become involved in the sport; as players, referees, officials, volunteers or just as enthusiastic spectators.

The reference to 'humble and hopeful beginnings', however, does not reflect the culturally significant force that women's football held in the early twentieth century across Europe. For example, around 1916 the Fédération des Sociétés Féminines Sportives de France (FSFSF) was founded and organised national championships; in England, the Dick, Kerr Ladies, established circa 1917, played internationally (Williams, 2013) to large crowds. These are just two instances amongst a plethora of woven histories relating to women's football which are often lost in new analyses of the game. Williams (2013) suggests there were approximately 150 women's football teams in the early 1920s but an associated governing body was not formed. This point acts as a reminder that women's football is not a 'new phenomena' or an 'emerging' force but rather a sport seeped in history which has been loved by many for over a century.

It is important to remember, however, that women's football has always been associated with criticism and in the past 'players have been accused of being unwomanly, of risking their physical health and of usurping resources reserved for men' (Hjelm, 2011, 143). Women's football has always been regulated either literally or socioculturally by others, for instance the FA's 50-year ban on women playing on League and affiliated football pitches (Williams, 2014) that stunted the development and visibility of women's football.

FIFA does make reference to the unequal history of the game and future challenges within their vision and strategy:

> FIFA's Women's Football Strategy will empower the organisation to take further concrete steps to address the historic shortfalls in resources and representation, while advocating for a global stand against gender discrimination through playing football.
>
> (FIFA, 2018, 4)

> Women's football continues to grow rapidly, but there is still a lot of work to be done to ensure all our member associations are fulfilling the true potential of the sport.
>
> (FIFA, 2019b, 5)

So how do these positive participation numbers and popularity of the game post-World Cup 2019 position women's football globally? The position, in short, is paradoxical.

The 'legacy of exclusion' (FIFPro, 2017, 10) rooted in women's football is not something which can be easily altered by successful world cups and increased participation numbers.

> Despite significant growth in the women's game and the role of women in football since the first FIFA Women's World Cup™ in 1991, the women's game has not yet realised its full potential.
>
> (FIFA, 2016, 36)

> The women's global game exists on a spectrum. A relatively small group of recognised professionals sit at one end, and a relatively large group of amateurs sit at the opposite end.
>
> (FIFPro, 2017, 8)

Countries who have achieved success on the world stage report drops in popularity and attendance after the World Cup fever passes; lower-league clubs in Germany are an example of this, however, the top clubs sustained momentum (Pfister et al., 2014). FIFA (2018, 4) themselves acknowledge that 'the game is both in rude health and in need of fundamental change' with stories of both progress and cultural stagnation being told 'at the same time' (Woodward, 2017, 690).[1] Despite the increased participation numbers women can only make a living from the game in 30 out of the 123 FIFA-listed countries (Agergaard and Tiesler, 2014).

England's performance in the 2019 World Cup has not forced socio-structural change as first hoped and even anticipated. After a year-long review, the men's Premier League decided not to take over the running of the WSL (McElwee, 2020a) as was initially reported (Ziegler, 2019). A decision which would seemingly satisfy the women's clubs who were reported as being against a Premier League take-over in favour of an independently run organisation (Carp, 2020). The devastation caused by Covid-19 in 2020 will have repercussions for individuals, societies and sport for decades to come. One of the first academic reviews of the pandemic in relation to women's elite football outlined concerns over the uncertainty of the elite game in connection to player well-being, contracts, investments and the general health of the sport (Clarkson et al., 2020). A controversial decision by the FA to cancel the remaining fixtures of the WSL (the men's Premier League resumed on 17th June 2020) due to Covid-19 was pre-empted by Wrack who reported on the perceived inequitable treatment of the women's game after the FA announced there would not be any funding support relating to the pandemic at this time (Wrack, 2020). Although, Director of Women's Football, Baroness Sue Campbell praised the developed infrastructure of the game for support at this time:

> Little was any of us to know that Covid-19 would enforce a hard stop on our season. It's only with the infrastructure we have in place that we can now begin to plan for the future.
>
> (FA, 2020b)

Later, however, the FA allowed the continuation of boys' elite football academies but not those of girls amidst the second national, English lockdown in November 2020 (McElwee, 2020b). The Premier League later announced support investment of over £1 million to assist the women's elite game to recover from the crisis (Daniels, 2020) but it is too early to know how this will truly impact the future of the game.

In *FIFA 2.0: The vision for the future* it is acknowledged that 'football has always reflected the culture of its time. And as society evolves, so does football' (2016, 12). This evolution, however, is one which is slow due to the entrenched cultural position of women's football within some countries globally. My previous work highlights this paradoxical situation by examining the pleasures girls and women gain from playing amidst gender stereotyping and prejudice, referred to as the *Sanctuary Paradox* (Pielichaty, 2020). Woodhouse and others' (2019) work on the ideological construction of the WSL reports the complexities linked to the FA ownership of the game in terms of structure and governance, noting they failed to take on board stakeholder needs and concerns.

Governing bodies have demonstrated an awareness of this continual perceptual and stereotypical stigma attached to women's football. For example, the FA's *Game Plan for Growth* strategy (2017) outlined eight priorities, one of which was to 'change perceptions and social barriers to participation and following' which showed a promising consideration of one of the underpinning, restricting factors to future development within England. This priority objective was measured one year on but focused on the brand of the game, ticket prices, social media and the 'Salute' campaign. It is difficult to fully analyse whether structural and cultural change was tackled by these actions. This comes at a time when Women in Football (2020) reported that 66% of women working in football have experienced gender discrimination of some kind.

The patriarchy of football within the UK is so deeply ingrained and synonymous with the sport that the campaigns, projects, activist stands need to be powerful, unyielding and uncompromising. The FA's 2017–2020 strategy focused on organisational targets which perhaps explain why perceptual change is lagging. The final chapter of this text will develop this notion further in connection to 'gender justice'. Ultimately 'there remains a pressing need for gender awareness in football research and policies' (Pfister, 2015a, 566), and the greater the examination of these issues, the greater chance of advancement.

For the love of the game

Oxenham documents the 'untold stories' of women's football and comments:

> Dozens of players across the world shared their stories and their time. Whether from Liverpool or Lagos, Tokyo or Kabul, Kingston or Paris, here's one thing that was always true: at an early age, they found the game and held on, driven neither by money nor fame – only the desire to be great.
>
> (Oxenham, 2017, xi)

The elite women players in Oxenham's collection shared a passion to succeed in professional football. Football, according to these players, was sometimes used as an escape from poverty, homelessness and war; a space to feel worthy; an emblem of success. Football helps to create and consolidate identities (Pielichaty, 2019) and also to make new friends (Themen and Van Hooff, 2017). Grundlingh (2010, 52) explains:

> What is clear is that the commitment and passion for the game sustains them and allows for self-expression in the sporting arena. Soccer is also a way for them to take control of their own leisure time. Ultimately, it signifies the degree of agency that these young women can assert through soccer.
>
> (Grundlingh, 2010, 52)

The sense of achievement girls and women gained through playing is important to note: professional player Fara Williams' connection to football is described as 'something she was good at, and that – being good at something – was powerful' (Oxenham, 2017, 68). Some players used football as a means to prove to the boys that they were worthy and could play well, describing football as 'relaxing, energetic, a chance to tackle people and *take your anger out* on something' (Pielichaty, 2015, 498). Players in these examples demonstrate a determination to participate and succeed in football; against the backdrop of the historical and continuing challenges to playing, women and girls are actively trying to normalise their football playing by creating a model of participation that accommodates their love for the sport (see Pielichaty, 2020).

The persistence of gender stereotyping can cause great difficulty in the quest for equality in sport; maintaining a traditional script of femininity and subservience can impact upon progression (Anderson, 2009). Girls in my earlier research focused on how to 'prove the boys wrong' about their footballing abilities and continuously compared their situation to boys' and men's football (Pielichaty, 2015). In my later work, players became more focused on their own 'football self' but continued to acknowledge their placement within the football hierarchy (Pielichaty, 2019). Furthermore, Harris' 2007 study exploring the gender identities of university women footballers reported that the women themselves accepted and therefore confirmed their subservient position in the game by allowing gender discrimination to occur. This is also relevant to previous work which questions the unsteady transformational stand girls and women can take in the game whilst continuing to normalise and tolerate inequality (Pielichaty, 2020).

Girls' and women's football globally

FIFA's (2019b, 7) report states that 'women's football continues to grow rapidly', with an estimated 30 million female players
worldwide (FIFA, 2016). The global picture of girls' and women's
football, however, is fragmented and layered. Different countries
around the world are at varying stages of development, and FIFA
(2019b, 7) acknowledges that 'there is still a lot of work to be done'.
Women footballers globally have been subject to 'crude stereotype
and malicious myth' (Mangan, 2004, 1) and often have to break
through gender barriers before they can gain any credibility or recognition (Hall, 2004). Each culture and community faces different
challenges to football participation and to varying degrees.

The dominant US team has long been associated with success
and leading the way in women's soccer in relation to credibility and
cultural acceptance. Although, at the time of writing the United
States Soccer Federation were legally challenged by the US team
on the grounds of alleged gender discrimination and equal pay and
have since requested up to $67 million in damages (Das, 2020). As
Kristiansen, Broch and Pedersen (2014) explain, the US's success at
the global level had not historically translated to sustained professional league success with many attempts folding since their first
World Cup win in 1991. 'Overall, women's professional soccer in the
US is promising but from a business perspective continues to struggle to find a foothold and sustainable growth in the domestic sport
market' (Kristiansen et al., 2014, 6). Since then the National Wom-
en's Soccer League (NWSL) has facilitated the women's game and
hosts nine teams within the league. It is reported that the league has
now moved beyond 'mere survival' due to increased broadcasting
and salaries (Dure, 2017). So how will the NWSL capitalise on the
US's recent World Cup victory? The NWSL saw a spike in attendance figures across the board after the national team's 2015 World
Cup win but these soon dropped after the hype died down, currently the Portland Thorns average 18,000 spectators a game but
other teams such as Reign FC achieve fewer than 4,000 a match
(Murray, 2019a).

Women's football in other countries across the world is much
less developed than America. For example, the Cameroon national
team's domestic leagues have been stopped several times: they lack
funding, resources and medical insurance (Enow, 2019). Girls' and
women's football in Cameroon is associated with 'school drop-
outs and delinquents' (Enow, 2019) indicating the social struggle

and fight that some players make to play and platform their sport. Engh's (2010) paper examining women's football in South Africa explains that footballers have been engaging and actively playing organised games for over 40 years but despite this are still expected to 'play like men but look like women' (Engh, 2010, 12). Furthermore, the South Africa Football Association Sanlam National Women's League was launched in 2001 and involved more than 300 teams providing a space for player development, identification and sponsorship buy-in. As the article explains, however, the 2004–2008 period of South African women's football was laden with setback and tragedy:

> As women's football became incorporated into SAFA structures following the Pickard Commission, it increasingly became victim of power struggles, fractional politics and male domination.
>
> (Engh, 2010, 16)

This period involved attempts to 'feminise' the women's game in South Africa, and national team players 'were made to attend etiquette classes and told to keep their hair long so as to appear feminine' (Engh, 2010, 17) which arguably indicates superficial change in an attempt to target cultural transformation. These efforts at feminisation were underlined by more sinister and brutal connections to racism, homophobia and sexism within South Africa which were viewed as relational to the rape and murder of Eudy Simelane, a former Banyana Banyana player in 2008 (Engh, 2010).

> In this complex terrain of simultaneous exclusion and inclusion from the sporting core, women footballers in South Africa continue to battle for centre stage.
>
> (Engh, 2010, 18)

This connection to paradoxical times of exclusion and inclusion resonates with previous work (Woodward, 2017; Pielichaty, 2020) and presents the multi-faceted position women occupy when carving out space to play within male-dominated societies.

Women's football is seen as taboo in India (Majumdar and Bandyopadhyay, 2005) and related to erotica in Brazil (Votre and Mourão, 2004). Fisher and Dennehy (2015) examined the embodied experiences of women football players in Brazil, and despite increased opportunities for women they are constrained by pressures to present idealised feminine bodies. This examination explains how the lawful prohibition of women from playing football in Brazil between 1941 and 1979 has gone on to shape the way in which women's football has been stigmatised within the country. The gender inequality in Brazilian football is thought to be a human rights issue whereby 'Brazilian football is utterly dominated by patriarchal institutions' (Knijnik and Horton, 2013, 62). Authorities in Brazil have previously enforced guidelines and parameters on women players in terms of their visual appearance and sexualised image, including the banning of cropped hair in favour of longer, preferably blonde styles (Knijnik and Horton, 2013). Brazilian women's football also has received unfavourable global press after team Taboao da Serra conceded 69 goals in four games demonstrating a discrepancy of standards (i, 2020, 2).

The Zambian players in Jeanes and Magee's (2014) study relished the new friendships they made through football but also acknowledged that their participation was not fully successful in tackling female subordination prevalent in their community. Despite struggling to challenge the patriarchal stronghold in their Zambian society, football did improve players' physical strength and fitness and provided them with a sense of belonging and hope. Girls' and women's participation in football is complicated and subject to both conformity and resistance to normative views of femininity. In Israel, football functions as a 'stronghold of masculinity' (Parets et al., 2011, 229). The Israeli football players as discussed by Parets et al. (2011) understood their participation to be a hobby for personal pleasure. They accepted that women's football was marginal and that women were negatively perceived as inferior to men – and therefore that women's football was second rate to the men's game.

In other areas of the world, Japan women won the World Cup in 2011 and are highly regarded by opposition and have made strides towards perceptual change in their nation but despite this their domestic set-up is reported to be limited due to having only two leagues organised on a part-time arrangement (Patrick, 2019). There are approximately 50,500 registered players in the Japanese Football Association compared with circa 2 million in the US which is also underpinned by lower numbers of female coaches nationally (Longman, 2019). Historically, Japanese players have migrated between countries depending on the success or failure of global leagues. For example, Sawa transferred from her Japanese club to the US and back again in between the suspension and start-up of the American leagues (Takahashi, 2014). Manzenreiter (2008) here explains how football in Japan is particularly difficult for women to penetrate whilst still offering a potential platform for transformation:

> Female subordination and male superiority are performed in everyday life, codified at political and administrative levels, exploited in economic relations and symbolically reproduced in popular cultural forms. But gender relations are far from being static, and football serves as one battle field for the reconstruction of the gender order in Japanese society.
>
> (Manzenreiter, 2008, 255)

This highlights the complexities of women's football amongst the cultural positioning which it takes. A change to this came in September 2020 when TRT World (2020) reported that Yuki Nagasato, on loan from Chicago Red Stars, signed for the men's team – Hayabusa Eleven, stating: 'I was really inspired by messages on gender gap by Rapinoe at the World Cup and I was wondering if I could also send a message to the society'.

Players in China were seen to be more successful and victorious than their male counterparts and 'have contradicted past and present stereotypes of femininity' (Hong and Mangan, 2003, 54). Although, according to Hong and Mangan, these perceptual changes have not impacted upon structural changes in the Chinese leagues with women earning considerably less than men, 'it remains a bitter irony that failed men (internationally) are rewarded far more handsomely than successful women (internationally)' (Hong and Mangan, 2003, 55). The achievements of the Chinese women's football team are thought to have empowered social change and have 'helped to reinforce gender evolution' (Hong and Mangan, 2003, 53). In 2016 the Chinese Football Association issued a plan to transform China's engagement and success in football and aimed for the women's team to be world-class by 2030 and in general to become 'a first-class football superpower' by 2050 (BBC, 2016). Alipay, a technology company, has pledged to invest $145 million to grow women's soccer over the next ten years and to reclaim some of its earlier successes, namely a semi-final place in the 1999 World Cup (Pham, 2019).

Football is the biggest participation sport for girls and women in Norway and Sweden, and Scandinavian countries are rated as pioneers of the women's game and in particular 'sports labour migration' into their clubs has been a topic of interest (Agergaard et al., 2013, 769). Although it has not always been that way as Svensson and Oppenheim (2018, 576) explain through the case study of Öxabäcks IF, the players associated with the club from 1966 to 1999 had to 'convince' stakeholders of football's significance and importance to the women who played. Hjelm (2011, 157) discusses the 'gendered inequality in Swedish football' which fuels society's opinion that women's football is technically inferior to the men's. Although, after the women's third place victory in the 2019 World Cup, the Swedish team were welcomed home by 30,000 fans in Gothenburg (Wrack, 2019b) demonstrating the appetite for women's football and momentum to build upon this success.

Women in and around football

Women and girls must still negotiate a complicated and labyrinthine pathway through to the world of sport, whether as a fan, official, player, manager, director or coach. Only 9% of executive members worldwide are female (FIFA, 2019b, 12) which demonstrates that increases in participation of the game have not dramatically affected the representation of women in senior positions. A 'boom', however, in executive membership in Germany and leadership successes in Norway has been reported (Strittmatter and Skirstad, 2017). There are pockets of transformative practice occurring in the sport but perhaps the widespread nature of change is still lacking. Alternative leadership roles, such as coaching, also position women as 'other', and male dominance, even within the women's game, is viewed as the norm (Fielding-Lloyd and Meân, 2011).

The visibility of women in management/head coach roles is improving, as reflected by the final of the World Cup in 2019 where Jill Ellis's US played Sarina Wiegman's Netherlands. Wiegman was one of just three Dutch women to receive the highest coaching qualification in football (Vissers, 2019), whereas Ellis was the first coach to win back-to-back World Cups in 81 years (Murray, 2019b). Successful accounts of female leadership on the world stage are highlighted by Hofmann et al. (2014) and since 2000 successful women Head Coaches have predominantly managed the US and German national teams. Despite this, the national football federations from across the globe are still dominated by men (Hofmann and Sinning, 2016), and in order to create more widespread change these isolated success stories need to become the 'new normal'.

Upon closer inspection of the experiences of women coaches in football, the cultural hurdles in which women must leap become apparent. Lewis et al. (2018) examine women's accounts of the coach education system in England and found that women felt underappreciated and pressured to prove themselves as worthy for the position. This is a finding that is also reflected in previous research of girls and women football players (Pielichaty 2015, 2020). Women coaches also recalled several occasions of experiencing 'abusive, derogatory or sexist language' (Lewis et al., 2018, 34) received from male coaches on the programme or by the education team themselves. Overall, these experiences are contributing to women 'finding it difficult to comprehend and integrate themselves in an established male-dominated coaching hierarchy' (Lewis et al., 2018, 37). Consistent with other patriarchal, hegemonic fields within society, access to participation and engagement for women is more straightforward than seeking to establish leadership and managerial roots within the industry.

Women spectators are still aware that the 'dominant cultural constructions of sports fandom are coded masculine' (Esmonde et al., 2015, 42) and their fandom is perceived as 'inauthentic' (Pope, 2016, 325). Spectator attendance at women's football games is complex, and Valenti et al.'s (2019, 1) study highlight a lack of continuous growth. They report that stadium attendance relates to five factors: stage of the competition, uncertainty of match outcome, competitive intensity, away club's reputation and weather conditions. Valenti et al. (2019, 10) also examined the rationale for attendance, whereby 'supporters of women's football are not driven by the quality of the competing teams. In contrast, they seem to be motivated to watch clubs with a brand that is recognisable from the men's game'.

This outcome is seemingly problematic for the future progression of the women's game which has sought to increase quality on the pitch in a bid to then produce a better 'product' for a wider audience. If the quality of the teams is irrelevant in comparison to a recognised branded club then the efforts of the organising bodies surrounding women's football appear to be marginalised. Performance and playing quality, therefore, is vital to the future of the sport, but stadium attendance, as documented by Valenti et al., appears to be driven by other factors.

Hallmann et al. (2018) investigated fan 'attachment' as a significant factor for attendance at women's football games across

Germany and Japan. They illustrate that attachment to the team, coach, country and women's sport in general was viewed as key for the spectator-sport relationship. Although the practical implications of this study can be questioned:

> When promoting matches, the love for the sport of football should be emphasized through athletes enjoying the game and spectators cheering happily for a team. This could include clear statement of young players highlighting the beauty of the game.
>
> (Hallmann et al., 2018, 916)

Hereby, women's football is encouraged to utilise 'softer' marketing techniques around fun, enjoyment and 'beauty' which is potentially patronising to the game. Players, who strongly identified with football, want women's football to be taken seriously and not promoted as a hobby or leisure pursuit (see Pielichaty, 2019). This will be discussed further in Chapter 4, whereby player needs to be considered credible and professional in both appearance and performance are explored. Highlighting the 'beauty' of the game by means of promoting match attendance does not seem to sit well with a need for gender justice and empowerment.

Media coverage of girls' and women's sport in general is still limited and lacking in terms of visibility and credibility. In the Netherlands there has been increased media coverage of women's football; however, the content of the coverage is entrenched by links to masculinity and men's football (Peeters and Elling, 2015). Women footballers are often 'infantilized' and sexualised by social media and not provided with the same quality and quantity of coverage as their male counterparts (Coche, 2016, 103). An analysis of media coverage of women's football in Germany as part of the 2011 World Cup demonstrated that reporting was 'gendered' and sexualised and players' femininities were drawn upon to frame the sport (Pfister, 2015b). In the following World Cup, Black and Fielding-Lloyd (2019) examined English national newspaper reports and found that 'outsiderness' was used to position women's football as separate to the men's game; in some cases, the examples used in the study expressed women's football as a patronising oddity, one report claimed:

> Women are perfectly able to play up and play the game just like men (even when they aren't cushioned by fat sponsorship deals,

and telephone-number salaries). ... Over the full 90 minutes, they didn't wilt in the 80F heat. Their legs lasted.

(Black and Fielding-Lloyd, 2019, 288)

On the contrary, Petty and Pope's (2019) analysis of the 2015 Women's World Cup reported positive engagement with the tournament, whereby the 'Lionesses' branding and terminology sought to provide an avenue for valuable connectivity through the media. Black and Fielding-Lloyd's (2019) work does acknowledge that most of the journalists reporting on the Women's World Cup were men but they do present an uplifting conclusion encouraging others to utilise positive memories from the 2015 World Cup to help shape future valuations of women's football.

There has been a noticeable increase in the number of women journalists in England reporting on the game for the 2019 Women's World Cup and on women's sport in general. In particular, the development of the *Telegraph Women's Sport* has been very worthy with pioneer Anna Kessel at the helm of the initiative that has helped to tackle inequality in women's sport coverage. Former footballer Alex Scott has asserted herself as a credible, professional and astute pundit for both the women's and men's game across major televised platforms, despite receiving much sexist abuse for her on-screen presence (Bech, 2019).

In relation to officiating, perceptions about ability are historically based on gender stereotypes and women's 'competence as football officials was questioned even before they had entered the field of play' (Forbes et al., 2016, 534). But times are changing: Bibiana Steinhaus was the first woman in Europe to regularly referee top-tier matches in the Bundesliga and a report claims, 'Steinhaus, is confident the players have completely accepted her authority. It is the wider world, she says, that may perceive her as a novelty' (Morgan, 2019b). Sian Massey-Ellis has been a very visible source of inspiration in football as both an international referee and in her role as Assistant Referee within the men's Premier League. Furthermore, Stéphanie Frappart officiated the UEFA men's Super Cup game between Liverpool and Chelsea (Wrack, 2019c) to much anticipation due to its European staging. The reports following the match were positive, although similar to those highlighted by Black and Fielding-Lloyd (2019) addressed earlier in this chapter, narratively positions women in and around football by surprise (see Burt, 2019 for example) and low expectations.

Positive developments are being made on and off the field of play, and the 2019 Women's World Cup can be viewed as a landmark tournament in terms of integrity, performance and quality. There is so much more to be done though, with every positive developmental step, there appears to be challenge, backlash and disorder which needs to be targeted by a multipronged approach to transformation. In head coaching and management for example, Hofmann et al. (2014, 30) explain that female role models needed to 'prove that this career is possible' and therefore visibility is a must in terms of future progress.

Conclusion

This chapter has brought together a brief but contemporary view of the girls' and women's football environment. There have been significant signs of improvement in some areas of the globe in terms of participation numbers, National Governing Body (NGB) buy-in and general public interest. Fisher and Dennehy's (2015) investigation encourages potential for empowerment and transformation: 'between the surfaces of constraint and limitation, there is agency and expression occurring within the fissures and cracks through physical bodily and emotional expression' (Fisher and Dennehy, 2015, 1006). Like the English players in my previous work, change comes from a pure pleasure for the game, friendships and persistence in playing (Pielichaty, 2020). In some nations worldwide, however, the increasing statistics around girls' and women's football is not converting into 'real' cultural change, and 'the increasing popularity and expansion of access and opportunities for women in football in Brazil are not automatically translating into positive outcomes' (Fisher and Dennehy, 2015, 998). Improvements in terms of standard in play and the involvement of women in football have been made, but these continue to be undermined by ideological constraints:

> The signs on the pitch are encouraging, with the increased involvement of women, but there is little evidence of any cultural shift towards a more inclusive sport and gendered hostility endures.
>
> (Woodward, 2017, 264)

It is these elements that will be addressed in the final chapter of the book with a focus on how these developments can be further established to empower acceptance and movement towards cultural change.

Note

1 Pielichaty, H., Pleasure and the Sanctuary Paradox: Experiences of Girls and Women Playing Soccer, International Review for the Sociology of Sport (55/6) pp. 788–806. Copyright © [2020] (Sage). doi:10.1177/1012690219857023.

References

Agergaard, S., Andersson, T., Carlsson, B. and Skogvang, B.O. (2013) Scandinavian women's football in a global world: migration, management and mixed identity. *Soccer and Society*, 14(6), 769–780.

Agergaard, S. and Tiesler, N.C. (eds.) (2014) *Women, soccer and transnational migration*. London: Routledge.

Anderson, E. (2009) *Inclusive masculinity: the changing nature of masculinities*. London: Routledge.

BBC (2016) China aims to become football superpower 'by 2050'. *BBC*, 11 April. Available from: https://www.bbc.co.uk/news/world-asia-china-36015657 [Accessed 23 July 2019].

Bech, D. (2019) Alex Scott vows to continue TV punditry despite sexist abuse on social media 'every single day'. *Independent*, 10 May. Available from: https://www.independent.co.uk/sport/football/premier-league/alex-scott-sky-sports-bbc-sport-tv-pundit-twitter-sexism-abuse-a8907511.html [Accessed 6 September 2019].

Black, J. and Fielding-Lloyd, B. (2019) Re-establishing the 'outsiders': English press coverage of the 2015 FIFA women's world cup. *International Review for the Sociology of Sport*, 54(3) 282–301.

Burt, J. (2019) Jurgen Klopp leads praise for Stephanie Frappart's performance in Uefa Super Cup. *The Telegraph*, 15 August. Available from: https://www.telegraph.co.uk/football/2019/08/15/jurgen-klopp-leads-praise-stephanie-frapparts-performance-uefa/ [Accessed 6 September 2019].

Carp, S. (2020) Report: most WSL clubs opposed to Premier League takeover. *SportsProMedia*, 15 July. Available from: https://www.sportspromedia.com/news/wsl-premier-league-takeover-clubs-opposed [Accessed 16 July 2020].

Clarkson, B.G., Culvin, A. Pope S. and Parry, K.D. (2020) Covid-19: reflections on threat and uncertainty for the future of elite women's football in England. *Managing Sport and Leisure*. doi:10.1080/23750472.2020.17 66377.

Coche, R. (2016) Promoting women's soccer through social media: how the US federation used Twitter for the 2011 World Cup. *Soccer and Society*, 17(1), 90–108.

Daniels, T. (2020) Women's football receives £1m boost from the Premier League. *Insider Sport*. Available from: https://insidersport. com/2020/07/01/womens-football-receives-1m-boost-from-the-premier-league/ [Accessed 1 July 2020].

Das, A. (2020) U.S. Women's soccer team sets price for ending lawsuit: $67 Million. *The New York Times*, 21 February. Available from: https://www.nytimes.com/2020/02/21/sports/soccer/uswnt-equal-pay-lawsuit.html [Accessed 20 December 2020].

Dure, B. (2017) A season on the brink: wide-open NWSL making strides as fifth year kicks off. *The Guardian*, 13 April. Available from: https://www.theguardian.com/football/2017/apr/13/nwsl-season-preview [Accessed 23 July 2019].

Engh, N.H. (2010) The battle for centre stage: women's football in South Africa. *Agenda*, 24(85), 11–20.

Enow, N. (2019) Cameroon meltdown was hard to watch but context is all important. *The Guardian*, 24 June. Available from: https://www.theguardian.com/football/2019/jun/24/cameroon-england-women-world-cup-2019-context-meltdown [Accessed 16 July 2019].

Esmonde, K., Cooky, C. and Andrews, D.L. (2015) "It's supposed to be about the love of the game, not the love of Aaron Rodgers' eyes": challenging the exclusions of women's sports fans. *Sociology of Sport Journal*, 32(1), 22–48.

FA (2017) *The Gameplan for Growth: the FA's Strategy for Women's and Girls' Football: 2017–2020*. Available from: file:///C:/Users/PC/Downloads/fawomensstrategydocfinal-13317%20(1).pdf   [Accessed   11 June 2019].

FA (2020a) *The Gameplan for Growth – the journey to double participation*. Available from: file:///C:/Users/PC/Downloads/the-gameplan-for-growth-review---participation.pdf [Accessed 12 June 2020].

FA (2020b) *The Gameplan for Growth the FA's strategy for women's and girls' football: 2017–2020 final review and report*. Available from: file:///C:/Users/PC/Downloads/the-gameplan-for-growth-final-review-and-report.pdf [Accessed 23 July 2020].

FA (2020c) Inspiring positive change: the FA's strategy for women's and girls' football: 2020–2024. Available from: https://thefabrochures.co.uk/19268_WOMENS_GIRLS_FOOTBALL_STRATEGY_2020-24/index.html [Accessed 22 October 2020].

Fielding-Lloyd, B. and Meân, L. (2011) 'I don't think I can catch it': women, confidence and responsibility in football coach education. *Soccer and Society*, 12(3), 345–364.

FIFA (2014) *Women's football survey*. Available from: https://resources. fifa.com/image/upload/fifa-women-s-football-survey-2522649.pdf?-cloudid=emtgxvp0ibnebltlvi3b [Accessed 11 June 2019].

FIFA (2016) *FIFA 2.0: the vision for the future*. Available from: https:// resources.fifa.com/mm/document/affederation/generic/02/84/35/01/ fifa_2.0_vision_e_neutral.pdf [Accessed 11 June 2019].

FIFA (2018) *Women's football strategy*. Available from: https://resources. fifa.com/image/upload/women-s-football-strategy.pdf?cloudid=-z7w21ghir8jb9tguvbcq [Accessed 10 June 2020].

FIFA (2019a) *FIFA Women's World Cup France 2019: global broadcast and audience report*. Available from: https://img.fifa.com/image/upload/ rvgxekduqpeo1ptbgcng.pdf [Accessed 28 October 2019].

FIFA (2019b) *Women's football member associations survey report 2019*. Available from: https://img.fifa.com/image/upload/nq3ensohyxpuxov covj0.pdf [Accessed 8 July 2020].

FIFA (2020) *New report highlights social and economic legacy left by FIFA Women's World Cup 2019*. Available from: https://www.fifa.com/ womensworldcup/news/new-report-highlights-social-and-economic-legacy-left-by-fifa-women-s-world-cup- [Accessed 10 July 2020].

FIFPro (2017) *2017 FIFPro global employment report: working conditions in professional women's football*. Available from: https://fifpro.org/ attachments/article/6986/2017%20FIFPro%20Women%20Football%20 Global%20Employment%20Report-Final.pdf [Accessed 15 May 2019].

Fisher, C.D. and Dennehy, J. (2015) Body projects: making, remaking, and inhabiting the woman's futebol body in Brazil. *Sport in Society*, 18(8), 995–1008.

Forbes, A., Edwards, L. and Fleming, S. (2016) 'Women can't referee': exploring the experiences of female football officials within UK football culture. *Soccer and Society*, 16(4), 521–539.

Grundlingh, M. (2010) Boobs and balls: exploring issues of gender and identity among women soccer players at Stellenbosch University. *Agenda: Empowering Women for Gender*, 24(85), 45–53.

Hall, M.A. (2004) The game of choice: girls' and women's soccer in Canada. In: Hong, F. and Mangan, J.A. (eds.) *Soccer, women, sexual liberation: kicking off a new era*. London: Frank Cass Publishers, 30–46.

Hallmann, K., Oshimi, D., Harada, M., Matsuoka, H. and Breuer, C. (2018) Spectators' points of attachment and their influence on behavioural intentions of women's national football games. *Soccer and Society*, 19(7), 903–923.

Harris, J. (2007) Doing gender on and off the pitch: the world of female football players. *Sociological Research Online*, 12(1). Available from: http://www.socresonline.org.uk/12/1/harris.html [Accessed 5 March 2015].

Hjelm, J. (2011) The bad female football player: women's football in Sweden. *Soccer and Society*, 12(2), 143–158.

Hofmann, A.R. and Sinning, S. (2016) From being excluded to becoming world champions: female football coaches in Germany. *The International Journal of the History of Sport*, 33(14), 1652–1668.

Hofmann, A. R., Sinning, S., Shelton, C., Lindgrend, E.-C. and Barker-Ruchtid, N. (2014) "Football is like chess – You need to think a lot": women in a men's sphere. National female football coaches and their way to the top. *International Journal of Physical Education*, 51(4), 20–32.

Hong, F. and Mangan, J.A. (2003) Will the 'Iron Roses' bloom forever? Women's football in China: changes and challenges. *Soccer and Society*, 4(2–3), 47–66.

i (2020) *Team conceded 69 goals in four games*. 19th November, p. 2.

Jeanes, R. and Magee, J. (2014) Promoting gender empowerment through sport? Exploring the experiences of Zambian female footballers. In: Schulenkorf, N. and Adair, D. (eds.) *Global sport-for-development: critical perspectives*. Basingstoke: Palgrave Macmillan, 134–154.

Knijnik, J. and Horton, P. (2013) 'Only beautiful women need apply': human rights and gender in Brazilian football. *Creative Approaches to Research*, 6(1), 60–70.

Kristiansen, E., Broch, T.B. and Pedersen, P.M. (2014) Negotiating gender in professional soccer: an analysis of female footballers in the United States. *Sport Management International Journal*, 10(1), 5–27.

Lewis, C.J., Roberts, S.J. and Andrews, H. (2018) 'Why am I putting myself through this?' Women football coaches' experiences of the Football Association's coach education process. *Sport, Education and Society*, 23(1), 28–39.

Longman, J. (2019) When Japan lost its crown, it found a reason to start over. *The New York Times*, 10 June. Available from: https://www.nytimes.com/2019/06/10/sports/10wwc-japan.html [Accessed 23 July 2019].

Lyons, E. (2019) Women's World Cup: How brands are leveraging a 'culturally relevant' moment. *Marketing Week*, 30 May. Available from: https://www.marketingweek.com/womens-world-cup-sponsorship/ [Accessed 5 July 2019].

Majumdar, B. and Bandyopadhyay, K. (2005) The gendered kick: women's soccer in Twentieth Century India. *Soccer and Society*, 6(2/3), 270–284.

Mangan, J.A. (2004) Managing monsters. In: Hong, F. and Mangan, J.A. (eds.) *Soccer, women, sexual liberation: kicking off a new era*. London: Frank Cass Publishers, 1–6.

Manzenreiter, W. (2008) Football in the reconstruction of the gender order in Japan. *Soccer and Society*, 9(2), 244–258.

McCaskill, S. (2019) FA Launches Women's Soccer Streaming Platform To Show 150 Live WSL Matches. *Forbes*, 6 August. Available from: https://www.forbes.com/sites/stevemccaskill/2019/08/06/fa-launches-womens-soccer-streaming-platform-to-show-150-live-wsl-matches/#68960e4d18ec [Accessed 6 September 2019].

McElwee, M. (2020a) Premier League will not be taking over WSL in near future, after a year-long review. *The Telegraph*, 12 February. Available from: https://www.telegraph.co.uk/football/2020/02/12/premier-league-will-not-taking-wsl-near-future-year-long-review/ [Accessed 18 March 2020].

McElwee, M. (2020b) Youth football embroiled in equality row as elite girls told to stop playing while male academies continue. *The Telegraph*, 5 November. Available from: https://www.telegraph.co.uk/football/2020/11/05/youth-football-embroiled-equality-row-elite-girls-told-stop/ [Accessed 11 November 2020].

Morgan, T. (2019a) Club record attendances predicted for Women's Football Weekend as interest in women's game continues to grow. *The Telegraph*, 16 November. Available from: https://www.telegraph.co.uk/football/2019/11/16/club-record-attendances-predicted-womens-football-weekend-interest/ [Accessed 18 March 2020].

Morgan, T. (2019b) Bibiana Steinhaus interview: Life as Europe's leading female referee in a male-dominated world. *The Telegraph*, 10 April. Available from: https://www.telegraph.co.uk/football/2019/04/10/bibiana-steinhaus-interview-life-europes-leading-female-referee/ [Accessed 6 September 2019].

Murray, C. (2019a) After a brilliant World Cup victory, US stars return to their day jobs. *The Guardian*, 11 July. Available from: https://www.theguardian.com/football/2019/jul/11/usa-womens-world-cup-nwsl-victory-parade [Accessed 23 July 2019].

Murray, C. (2019b) 'The timing is right': Jill Ellis to resign after helming USA's World Cup double. *The Guardian*, 30 July. Available from: https://www.theguardian.com/football/2019/jul/30/jill-ellis-stepping-down-uswnt-coach [Accessed 1 August 2019].

Oxenham, G. (2017) *Under the lights and in the dark: untold stories of women's soccer*. London: Icon Books.

Parets, S., Levy M. and Galily, Y. (2011) National and gender identity perceptions among female football players in Israel. *Soccer and Society*, 12(2), 228–248.

Patrick, P. (2019) The rise and stall of women's football in Japan. *The Guardian*, 10 June. Available from: https://www.theguardian.com/football/when-saturday-comes-blog/2019/jun/10/womens-world-cup-rise-stall-football-japan [Accessed 16 July 2019].

Peeters, R. and Elling, A. (2015) The coming of age of women's football in the Dutch sports media, 1995–2013. *Soccer and Society*, 16(5–6), 620–638.

Petty, K. and Pope, S. (2019) A new age for media coverage of women's sport? An analysis of English media coverage of the 2015 FIFA Women's World Cup. *Sociology*, 53(3), 486–502.

Pfister, G. (2015a) Assessing the sociology of sport: on women and football. *International Review for the Sociology of Sport*, 50(4/5), 563–569.

Pfister, G. (2015b) Sportswomen in the German popular press: a study carried out in the context of the 2011 Women's Football World Cup. *Soccer and Society*, 16(5–6), 639–656.

Pfister, G., Klein, M.L. and Tiesler, N.C. (2014) Momentous spark or enduring enthusiasm? The 2011 FIFA Women's World Cup and its impact on players' mobility and on the popularity of women's soccer in Germany. In: Agergaard, S. and Tieseler, N.C. (eds.) *Women, soccer and transnational migration*. London: Routledge, 140–158.

Pham, S. (2019) Alipay is investing $145 million to grow women's soccer in China. *CNN*, 8 July. Available from: https://edition.cnn.com/2019/07/08/business/alipay-china-women-soccer/index.html [Accessed 23 July 2019].

Pielichaty, H. (2015) 'It's like equality now; it's not as if it's the old days': an investigation into gender identity development and football participation of adolescent girls. *Soccer and Society*, 16(4), 493–507.

Pielichaty, H. (2019) Identity salience and the football self: a critical ethnographic study of women and girls in football. *Qualitative Research in Sport, Exercise and Health*, 11(4), 527–542.

Pielichaty, H. (2020) Pleasure and the sanctuary paradox: Experiences of girls and women playing soccer. *International Review for the Sociology of Sport*, 55(6), 788–806.

Pope, S. (2016) Female fans of men's football. In: Hughson, J. Maguire, J., Moore, K. and Spaaij, R. (eds.) *Routledge handbook of football studies*. London: Routledge, 325–335.

Sport England (2020) Women's football given £1m boost. Available from: https://www.sportengland.org/news/womens-football-given-1m-boost [Accessed 24 July 2020].

Strittmatter, A.M. and Skirstad, B. (2017) Managing football organizations: a man's world? comparing women in decision-making positions in Germany and Norway and their international influence: a contextual approach. *Soccer and Society*, 18(1), 81–101.

Svensson, D. and Oppenheim, F. (2018) Equalize it!: 'sportification' and the transformation of gender boundaries in emerging Swedish women's football, 1966–1999. *The International Journal of the History of Sport*, 35(6), 575–590.

Takahashi, Y. (2014) Nadeshiko: international migration of Japanese women in world soccer. In: Agergaard, S. and Tieseler, N.C. (eds.) *Women, soccer and transnational migration*. London: Routledge, 102–116.

Themen, K. and Van Hooff, J. (2017) Kicking against tradition: women's football, negotiating friendships and social spaces. *Leisure Studies*, 36(4), 542–552.

TRT World (2020) *Japanese female football star Yuki Nagasato joins men's team*. Available from: https://www.trtworld.com/sport/japanese-female-football-star-yuki-nagasato-joins-men-s-team-39998 [Accessed 15 October 2020].

UEFA (2016) *Women's football across the national associations 2016/17.* Available from: https://www.uefa.com/MultimediaFiles/Download/OfficialDocument/uefaorg/Women'sfootball/02/43/13/56/2431356_DOWNLOAD.pdf [Accessed 11 June 2019].

UEFA (2017) *Women's football across the national associations 2017.* Available from: https://www.uefa.com/MultimediaFiles/Download/OfficialDocument/uefaorg/Women'sfootball/02/51/60/57/2516057_DOWNLOAD.pdf [Accessed 11 June 2019].

UEFA (2019a) *Nike on the ball with exclusive UEFA Women's Football deal.* Available from: https://www.uefa.com/insideuefa/about-uefa/administration/marketing/news/newsid=2594980.html [Accessed 5 July 2019].

UEFA (2019b) *Women's football.* Available from: https://www.uefa.com/insideuefa/football-development/womens-football/ [Accessed 11 June 2019].

Valenti, M., Scelles, N. and Morrow, S. (2019) The determinants of stadium attendance in elite women's football: evidence from the UEFA women's champions league. *Sport Management Review.* doi:10.1016/j.smr.2019.04.005.

Vissers, W. (2019) Women's World Cup 2019 team guide no 20: Netherlands. *The Guardian,* 5 June. Available from: https://www.theguardian.com/football/2019/jun/05/womens-world-cup-2019-team-guide-no-20-netherlands [Accessed 1 August 2019].

Votre, S. and Mourão, L. (2004) Women's football in Brazil: progress and problems. In: Hong, F. and Mangan, J.A. (eds.) *Soccer, women, sexual liberation: kicking off a new era.* London: Frank Cass Publishers, 264–278.

Williams, J. (2013) *Globalising women's football: Europe, migration and professionalization.* Peter Lang: Bern.

Williams, J. (2014) *A contemporary history of women's sport, part one: sporting women, 1850–1960.* London: Routledge.

Women in Football (2020) *Women in Football launch new phase of growth as two thirds of members working in the industry report gender discrimination.* Available from: https://www.womeninfootball.co.uk/news/2020/10/08/new-phase-of-growth-as-66-per-cent-of-members-working-in-the-industry-report-gender-discrimination/ [Accessed 15 October 2020].

Woodhouse, D., Fielding-Lloyd, B. and Sequerra, R. (2019) Big brother's little sister: the ideological construction of women's super league. *Sport in Society,* 22(12), 2006–2023.

Woodward, K. (2017) Women's time? Time and temporality in women's football. *Sport in Society,* 20(5–6), 689–700.

Wrack, S. (2018) Sponsorship milestone shows women's football is now big business. *The Guardian,* 11 December. Available from: https://www.theguardian.com/football/blog/2018/dec/11/sponsorship-uefa-womens-football-business [Accessed 5 July 2019].

Wrack, S. (2019a) Barclays unveiled as women's super league sponsor in groundbreaking deal. *The Guardian,* 20 March. Available from: https://

www.theguardian.com/football/2019/mar/20/barclays-womens-super-league-sponsor-record-deal-uk-fa [Accessed 5 July 2019].

Wrack, S. (2019b) Sweden's Kosovare Asllani: '30,000 people came to celebrate our medal'. *The Guardian*, 12 July. Available from: https://www.theguardian.com/football/2019/jul/12/sweden-kosovare-asllani-30000-people-womens-world-cup-england [Accessed 23 July 2019].

Wrack, S. (2019c) Stéphanie Frappart takes centre stage in big moment for women in football. *The Guardian*, 13 August. Available from: https://www.theguardian.com/football/2019/aug/13/referee-stephanie-frappart-assistants-breaking-new-ground [Accessed 6 September 2019].

Wrack, S. (2020) Hollow promises of equality are to blame if women's super league is cancelled. *The Guardian*, 23 May. Available from: https://www.theguardian.com/football/blog/2020/may/23/hollow-promises-of-equality-are-to-blame-if-womens-super-league-is-cancelled [Accessed 1 July 2020].

Ziegler, M. (2019) Premier league could take control of women's super league. *The Times*, 3 July. Available from: https://www.thetimes.co.uk/article/record-audience-of-11-7m-proves-why-terrestrial-tv-is-vital-to-growth-of-women-s-football-q07338mpl [Accessed 5 July 2019].

3   The football self

The football self is the term I will use to describe the meaning football has to those who play in relation to their identity and self-understanding. It is the in-depth relationship between player and football. In this chapter I will personally position the football self before reporting my empirical findings of the football self. This chapter is based on two of my published articles: 'Identity Salience and the Football Self'[1] in *Qualitative Research in Sport, Exercise and Health* (Pielichaty, 2019) and also 'Pleasure and the Sanctuary Paradox'[2] published in the *International Review for the Sociology of Sport* (Pielichaty, 2020) which I have utilised and developed for the purposes of this book.

It is useful to begin this discussion with some of my own memories and historical artefacts. My mum recently found an old journal from my childhood in which I described what I thought was an unusual hobby in which I wrote: 'Football (I'm a girl)'. Part of the purpose of this book is to understand whether it is still deemed unusual for a 10-year-old girl to participate in football. I wonder whether the meaning of the football self has changed now? This chapter investigates this further.

By the age of 12, my own love for football remained untouched, as the following memory snippet describes:

> It was 'non-uniform' day at school, a chance to socially express oneself through a self-selected sartorial choice. I was delighted with my chosen attire: I was covered head-to-toe in Adidas sportswear, including the added extras of an Adidas necklace and socks. To me this semblance epitomised my identity at the time, that of footballer and tomboy. I was comfortable in my tracksuit in the knowledge that I could sprint anywhere I needed to at the drop of a hat. Speed was my strength on the pitch. Although, I wasn't on the pitch at this time, I was in a

French lesson and my identity as footballer was sat physically and socially amongst Languages textbooks and friends who were all expressing their own, (in)dependent identities. This was exactly the point. Being a footballer didn't stop as you left the changing rooms on a wet Sunday afternoon; it stayed with you, permeating the walls of home, school and sports halls. The football self, if worn strictly, wasn't a badge of honour or an outfit choice but in fact was attached to you, like giving a family member a constant 'piggy-back'. It was a fond functional and emotional accompaniment to self.

This extract helps to introduce the football self before I position it in a broader academic context. The extant literature theorising football identities, either in relation to boys' or girls' football are relatively few. More commonly, studies have focused on gender identity in general in relation to girls' and women's football (Renold, 2005; Harris, 2007; Jeanes, 2011; Gledhill and Harwood, 2015) but not specifically on girls' and women's *football* identities. My work provides an original perspective on what football means to the girls and women who play, through the analytic distinction of 'contingent' and 'salient' football selves as will be explored in this chapter.

Theories of identity

At this juncture it is important to frame the academic perspectives I utilise to interpret and analyse the data collected through my empirical study. These have predominantly stemmed from socio-psychology which complements my own educational background in psychology, philosophy and sport. The exploration and understanding of identity has currency in debates across a number of disciplines and subject areas. Identity is a 'widely used term across the social sciences and humanities' (Wagg et al., 2009, 119) with each area having its own focus or discussion entry point. Broadly speaking, identity concerns who we are and how we think about ourselves.

The socio-psychological concepts linked to Burke and Stets' (2009) theory of identity and Curry's (1998) web of selves have been utilised to offer insight into what football means to the girls and women who play with regard to self-understanding. Curry conceptualises identities as multiple and understands them as operating within a 'complex web of selves' which shift and change depending on context and time. This theorisation stems from psychology, but one that is more accommodating of the social world in which identities manoeuvre. The web of selves conceptualisation provides a view of identity management that places greater emphasis on individual agency:

> Not surprisingly, adolescents have been found to maintain a complex web of selves to help accommodate the complexities of modern living – with different 'selves' featuring in the family, at school or with friends.
>
> (Curry, 1998, 109)

This position arises from an examination of adolescent identity in connection with social identity theory, and although only contributing to a small part of Curry's analysis, it provides useful insight for my take on identities in sport.

Although the web of selves conceptualisation is useful to ascertain fluidity of selves, when applying it to my earlier work (Pielichaty, 2015) it did not allow for an examination of 'why' these selves changed and what they meant to the players. This explains why Burke and Stets (2009) theory of identity has been introduced to accompany the web of selves concept to assist in examining the operational side of self-understanding in relation to football playing. Identity, for Burke and Stets, links to the meaning individuals place on particular roles and groups in society, and therefore, identity is inextricably linked to society, demonstrating overlap with Curry's theorisation. The reason why Burke and Stets' theorisations are significant is because they view identities in hierarchical form and understand selves to be managed by individuals in relation to identity prominence and commitment levels. Identities, for Burke and Stets (2009), can be multiple and operate simultaneously but do so in a hierarchical manner, linking to the salience of a particular identity:

> If more than one identity is activated in a situation, we expect that the identity with the higher level of prominence, or the identity with the higher level of commitment, will guide behaviour more than an identity with a lower level of prominence or commitment.
>
> (Burke and Stets, 2009, 133)

In this sense, the concept of identity allows for more prominent or salient identities (Stryker, 1968) to dominate at a given time and context due to higher commitment levels, which guide behaviour.

By using Burke and Stets' theory of identity in combination with the web of selves concept, the 'how' and 'why' players organised their selves around participation can be examined. In relation to the terminology adopted within this book, the concepts of football identity and football self will be used frequently and synonymously to be understood as self-understanding in connection with football participation. This book does however prioritise the terms 'self' and 'football self' because, unlike the term identity, which is 'riddled with ambiguity, riven with contradictory meanings, and encumbered by reifying connotations' (Cooper, 2005, 75), these concepts are not as semantically contested.

The football self: contingent and salient selves

Findings from my empirical research cohere around the concepts of what I term, respectively, the 'contingent football self' and the 'salient football self'. Players with contingent football selves enjoyed multiple sports, played for fun and viewed football participation as recreational rather than serious. 'Contingent' was specifically chosen to reflect the nature of football participation as dependent on context and other social activities taking place. These players organised their multiple identities in a fluid and shifting pattern, similarly to Curry's (1998) socio-psychological *web of selves* conceptualisation. Unlike Donnelly and Young's (1988) regimented four-step process to identity construction and confirmation, these players' selves changed and moved depending on what they were experiencing and in what context.

It is the players with contingent football selves who directly compared to the adolescent players in my very early work on girls' football identities and gender (Pielichaty, 2015); football featured as part of their current identities but did not dominate other selves. These players could be likened to the 'weekenders' in Lester's (2004) examination of mountaineering. Like the weekenders, players with contingent football selves enjoyed football but were not defined by it. At the other end of the spectrum, players with salient football identities were serious about football, dedicated to the sport and formed a time-limited constant football self. This conceptualisation and the term salience/salient is adapted from Burke and Stets' (2009) theorisation in relation to higher status identities which were driven by commitment levels. Players with salient football selves also demonstrated characteristics connected to one of the key qualities of 'serious leisure', namely 'strong identification' (Stebbins, 2008, 12).

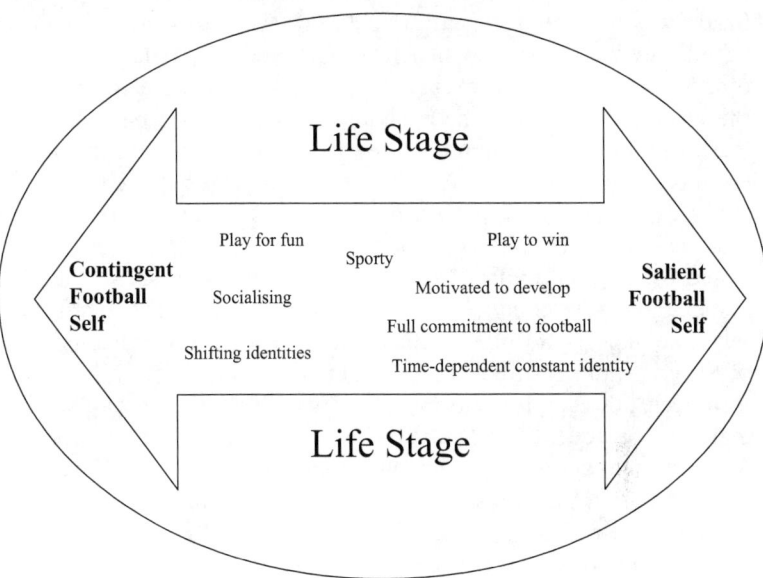

Figure 3.1 The Football Self Continuum (sourced from Pielichaty, 2019, 535).

These concepts are illustrated in the following figure where contingent and salient football selves have been placed on a Football Self Continuum (Figure 3.1).

The Football Self Continuum was not restrictive; players did not have to occupy and remain in one place on the continuum, rather it allowed for movement and change. Players with salient football selves were noted as having a 'time-dependent' constant identity which meant these players devoted all their energies and commitment to football for a certain length of time. During this time, these players reported being totally committed to football, were dedicated to achieve and excel in the game and prioritised participation above all else. These characteristics emerged through observations and conversations with the players and their family members. These seemingly constant football identities started to move and shift when the players entered new or different life stages and started to consider lifestyle changes such as going to university, starting a family or developing/progressing a career. Standpoint epistemology (Sprague, 2016) is useful to interpret this changing perspective of experiences, in which the location of the players in relation to their life stage changes, this therefore impacts on their understanding of self. The concern about playing football in the future was presented in Jeanes' (2005) research in which girls believed they would have to sacrifice their football participation for other more pressing commitments, such as starting a family. At these transitional times the normally high-status football identity had to adapt and accommodate new lifestyle priorities for the players. These life stages constituted a key element within the Football Self Continuum, they provided the context which continuously modified and interacted with the footballer's sense of self. As illustrated by the continuum there are certain characteristics that are associated more strongly with either a contingent or salient football self. The majority of players did noticeably align towards one end of the continuum more than the other. There was overlap in some instances, however, for example, players with salient football selves may also be considered 'sporty'. The continuum therefore allows for movement across the spectrum which, as already noted, will be impacted upon by life stages and individual circumstances.

Due to the fluidity in which the selves operated it was not possible from previous research to pinpoint the precise time or location in which the football self developed. It is possible though to make some inferences regarding the noticeable development of the football self based on observations and discussions during fieldwork exploration. All players initially engaged with their football identities nearer the contingent football self on the continuum; this may have been when they were first introduced to the game and indeed experimented with it as a new sport. As explained by Harriet (U9):

> I don't want to keep on playing football because my dream for a long time is to be a pop star like Katy Perry.

It was only at a later stage when players began to play football more regularly as part of a school team or sports club in which movement along the Football Self Continuum began to shift. Players with more contingent football selves were more likely to move in and out of football participation as it suited them. Players within the academy set-up had all started to transition from the contingent football self due to their involvement with the academy structure. Some of the younger players however were still involved in multiple sports or identified with a general 'sporty' persona, and therefore, their full movement across to salient football self may develop further. All players, regardless of their positioning along the continuum, demonstrated a passion for football. It was, however, the motivation to progress and develop within the sport which typified the players with a salient football self. Football salience was reinforced by winning competitions, going to national trials or becoming a regular feature in the starting 11 team. Having a passion for the sport was not an indicator of a salient football self per se, salience rather required a commitment to the sport and a drive to progress developmentally.

For some players football was one of many different sports in which they participated, for example, the U11 girls at the academy were also involved with netball, table-tennis, tag rugby, tennis, cricket and taekwondo. Football was often ranked as the second favourite sport in which the players at the school sites participated. The concept of fluid *sporting identities* (see, for example, Jeanes, 2005, 2011) is valuable because it provides the analytic tool to understand the multiplicity of sporting selves. It also supports the position that contemporary 'ideal girlhood is constantly being re-written' (Bettis and Adams, 2005, 9), depending on context. The players who took part in many other activities and sports presented a fluid sporting identity that often translated to a contingent football self.

Sian (U11), however, a player with a salient football self, believed that being regarded as 'sporty' accommodated her football playing very neatly. It is important to note that the Football Self Continuum allows for movement across the spectrum and merging of football self characteristics which depended upon the individual player. The biggest descriptor of self presented in a participatory activity was that of *sporty girl*. This was a category of girl to which Jodie (U17) related, and she explained that her friends at school were all sporty girls or non-girlie girls. Shifting from sport to sport meant they did not commit fully to football alone. The players themselves recognised that some girls were more committed to football than were others:

> I do football but I don't do like loads of football and I don't commit my life to it. Like compared to other people who focus on football and that's what they want to do and that's how they identify themselves.
>
> (Pauline, School U15)

The reason why girls played football varied from player to player. Some played to get out of lessons, some liked the fitness and competitive side of the sport and for others it was enjoyable and an area in which they achieved success (School U13). The personal connection to the football self was likened to a spider diagram, as discussed by these players (School U13):

> **Sophie**: It's like a spider diagram when you think about it, like there's you then there's like the things that come off like that [imitates drawing a spider diagram] makes you you.
>
> **HP**: So in your spider diagram you're in the middle and football is just one of the things that's coming off your diagram.
>
> **Sophie**: Yeah and then you'd have like other things coming off it like the reasons why you like it and what it is to you and everything.
>
> **HP**: Right that's really good Sophie, I'd like to think about that. Does anyone else's spider diagram have you and then there's football right in the middle?
>
> **Emma**: Well yeh because it's like every day..I like..because like me and my dad don't have that much in common it's like something that you bond with. So like we do summit like literally every day to do with football and it's like a part of my life that I've always done since I was little.
>
> **HP**: So you see it as really important because it's for bonding with your family as well?
>
> **Emma**: yeh
>
> **HP**: Stacey what about you? You said you see yourself and football in the middle, why's that?
>
> **Stacey**: Because it's sort of mostly all I do. It's just something I really like to do and hopefully it's what I will do in the future.

Sophie articulated the fluidity of identities in relation to football participation. For some players, football was one of many different activities in which they were involved, and therefore, football was interchangeable with other sports and social activities alongside the other moveable selves, which was consistent with Curry's web of selves concept and the adolescent girls' experiences of football participation in my previous study (Pielichaty, 2015). The 'complex web of selves' as articulated by Curry was similar to the spider diagram as illustrated by these players. Each aspect or self 'coming off it' (spider diagram) represented a mesh and fluidity between varying selves within changeable social contexts as consistent with Curry's research. A player's connection to football was demonstrated by where they placed football in their personal spider diagrams, this in turn highlighted what football meant to those girls. The social aspect of this positioning was demonstrated by Emma in relation to bonding with her father and the use of football participation as a shared activity. Similarly to Curry's web, the spider diagram illustration allowed the players to position themselves in different relational capacities to football, whether it be 'you' in the central role like Sophie or 'football' in the core position such as Stacey. These more interchangeable and fluid selves often connected to a more contingent football self. In contrast, Stacey and Emma explained that football was core to their identity and maintained a central position on their spider diagram due to the way it extended into their family life and future plans; these players had salient football selves. Jenny, an older player, drew parallels with this spider diagram concept and explained 'football was there in the centre and then whatever I did revolved around it'. More recently, however, Jenny discussed her enjoyment of new sports and activities and a movement away from a pure football focus which demonstrated the need to understand the football self as a continuum influenced by life stages. This resonates with my own football self: when I played for Lincoln City Ladies FC and West Bromwich Albion (WBA) Women FC my football self operated in a salient position but then the life stages of university, work and then starting a family affected my football self.

For some footballers who demonstrated a salient football self, football was part of their identification process and helped to create and form their self-understanding (see Burke and Stets, 2009):

I'm the twin who plays football; like that's been my identity. I've really realised it this year particularly because I've realised when I meet new people one of the first things I say is *I'm a football player.*

(Suzie)

For these players, football provided the principal, or even only space in which they felt they achieved and excelled. Kirsty (U11) joked that at school she was only 'good at P.E and break'. Esme (U15) claimed that 'I'm always happy when I play football' and equated well-being and satisfaction with participation. Alysha (U17) noted 'I've never stopped playing football' and that she could not imagine her life without it. For Sian (U11) football was 'the only thing I can really do, I'm not very good at Maths or English' and classed football as her 'main ability'. Football playing offered a sense of achievement and success to the players, which some had not experienced in other aspects of their lives. This is consistent with previous experiences of footballers who found achieving and excelling at sport as 'powerful' to their sense of worth (Oxenham, 2017). Players with salient football selves, who isolated football as the 'only' thing to focus their efforts on found football participation formed a very significant part of their self-understanding.

Players who dedicated more time to playing and showed higher levels of commitment placed football playing in a hierarchical position above other identities which they negotiated. This aligned to Burke and Stets' (2009) theory of identity which was useful in analysing those players who placed football at the core of their lives: players with a salient football self. The girls and women were committed and passionate about football and enjoyed the benefits of friends and teammates that their football 'membership' afforded them. Football identities were displayed more prominently in players who showed talent in and dedication to football in a way which consumed other areas of their lives; this was the majority of club-level and academy players. For example, for Christmas Catherine (U9) received many football-related gifts including an Old Trafford puzzle, an Eric Cantona kit and Manchester United boxer shorts, bath robe and calendar, which contributed to her 'materialistic identification' (Allen-Collinson and Hockey, 2007). Catherine explained that the shop did not produce Manchester United underwear for girls so she had received the male equivalent. Catherine's football identity thus extended beyond her football participation and into her home life which coheres with Stone's (2007) acknowledgement that football culture is expressed through everyday acts and routines which extend into home and work spaces. As demonstrated by Catherine, football for players with salient selves dominated their existence and the football self often transcended various social contexts which impacted upon their daily lives, as acknowledged by Stone (2007, 181) the 'activity space of football' is far reaching. When asked what she would do if she were never allowed to play football again, for example, Debbie (U15 School) replied, 'I would cry in a box for the rest of my life'. Sabine, an older player, explained she was never able to disconnect herself from football. Charlotte (U9) played for three football teams, two girls' teams and one boys' team; football constituted a significant part of her life as recalled by her father.

Players who demonstrated a salient football self often carved out frequent opportunities to play football, as explained by Kelly (U13):

> **HP**: What did you so this Saturday with your day off [the match had been cancelled]?
> **Kelly**: Football.

HP: You still played?
Kelly: Yes with my next-door-neighbour.

Sian (U11) demonstrated similar commitment by playing sports at home and frequently practising her skills outside of the formal football set-up. Her dad explained that she would prepare her football kit on Friday night and would be up early on Saturday ready to go. Stacey (School U13) articulated her love of football as 'just me' and believed it was her identity and important to who she was, describing that 'I play football almost every day of the week so there's nothing else'. A salient football identity was not necessarily linked to an increased enjoyment, passion or pleasure for the sport; but rather players who played for fun could be differentiated from the more serious players on the grounds of self-perceived commitment and dedication levels. Professional player, Sarah, described her childhood experience:

> Yeah I think they [other teammates] played for fun. I didn't; I played to win. It's weird because I love the game and I'm really passionate about it but I don't play for fun.

Players with salient football selves focused on football absorption, commitment with football almost being an occupation rather than a hobby or leisure pursuit, similar to Stebbins' description of 'leisure career' (2008, 5). Stebbins described the attributes involved in engaging with *serious leisure*, and the notions of preoccupation and commitment are entangled within this. This similarly connects to Donnelly and Young's (1988, 225) confirmation of identity stage which includes the cementing and development of the individuals 'subcultural career'.

Both Lucy and Kelly (U13s) agreed that their social lives had to work around football and discussed not having 'sleep-overs' at friends' houses because football dominated their everyday lives. Sleep-overs, which often took place on weekends, were not feasible due to the pressures of getting to sleep early on Saturday to feel refreshed and prepared ahead of the Sunday football game. The web of selves concept does not work for players with salient identities as they could not easily disengage from their football self within different, shifting social contexts. The web allows for interconnected selves to fluidly move and interlock in a relational way to the social environment around them; however, the salient football self does not offer this fluidity of movement but instead remains connected to football across a variety of social contexts. Craig explained that football was part of who his daughter was and was in full support of nourishing her football identity through extra football sessions and financial support. Another father, Peter, was aware of the extent to which his daughter Olive (U13) was influenced by football and explained that it became a controlling factor over other things she did. Olive's first Manchester United shirt was framed on her bedroom wall, and she had posters on her wall of both men and women footballers at home. Peter explained that football was Olive's identity, sometimes to her detriment due to the way in which she was conscious of her diet in relation to her athletic and physical development. The salient football self extended into home life and occupied the players' everyday activities and pleasures. Graeme described his daughter's relationship with football as obsessive and that it was far more extreme than her brother's love of football. He explained, 'I would be very surprised if she fell out of love with football purely because it's such a big part of her life'.

Burke and Stets' (2009) interpretation of 'identity theory' states that identities can be multiple, identities are organised and hierarchical but the status of these can change, identities operate at conscious and unconscious levels and identity and identities are affected by behaviour and choice. It was clear that the players who operated with a fluid, shifting web of selves, created time and space for their football playing alongside their other identities. These contingent players' football identities were indeed multiple but were not placed in a hierarchical position in relation to their other identities, thus standing in contrast to the concept of 'low level' and 'higher level' identities as originally formulated by Burke and Stets (2009, 136). This was exemplified by Rebecca (School U13), who argued that if she had a choice to play football on Wednesday or have a free manicure then she would choose the manicure. For these girls Curry's web of selves was applicable and these players slotted football playing into their everyday lives alongside other activities. Jodie (U17) explained that some girls at school only played football to 'fit in' and to get out of lessons; here Jodie distinguished via 'vocabularic identification' (Allen-Collinson and Hockey, 2007) – her more committed, salient football identity – from those more ad hoc players.

There was noted to be a discrepancy between players with salient football selves and those with more contingent football selves when they played together in educational settings. Alysha (U17) expressed frustration when playing for her school team because other girls 'just play it for fun', whereas Alysha viewed the sport as a career path to future success. This was similar to Zoe (U17) who explained the irritation she felt about the lack of quality in her college football team. Zoe was very committed to football and had been for international trials and was determined to make a career of the sport. Any footballing experiences impacted upon her both emotionally and physically:

> **Zoe:** If I don't play well I just sit there and look out of the window the whole way home and won't talk to anybody, headphones are put back in. And then, ..., when I get home I'll go back upstairs and not talk to anyone for the rest of the day.
> **HP:** So does it affect you for that long then?
> **Zoe:** Oh yeah, it just sort of knocks you back quite a bit.

Zoe's football self seemed to be experienced, not as changeable or dynamic but as highly consistent and operated as a constant identity that affected Zoe's football and home life experiences. As part of Zoe's 'socialization' stage (Donnelly and Young, 1988) she was consolidating her position as serious footballer by choosing to act in this manner when confronted by a poor individual performance.

The mobile football self

Football selves, however, do change and shift when the club players progress through different life stages and are faced with educational- and family-based decisions:

> I remember going to training one night, ..., and then kinda realised on the way home, I was driving home, quite late at night, thinking, kinda, this just isn't for me anymore.
>
> (Michelle)

> I want to carry on playing but I think I'm gonna play for more of a village team or a reserve team coz I wanna do A-Levels and then go to uni and I think that's maybe a bit more important now.
>
> (Jodie, U17)

Michelle referred to the moment she lost her interest and commitment to football, her previously constant identity began to shift to something more fluid and changeable. Moreover, Jodie explained that educational changes and prioritising university prospects would impact upon her future football participation. This is consistent with previous research which argued that young people are aware of life transitions, including educational transitions (Allen-Collinson and Brown, 2012), and these are important to them (Valentine, 1997; Wyn et al., 2011). Moreover, these changes in life stages do connect to Donnelly and Young's 'Acceptance/ Ostracism' phase in terms of the players confirming their identity as a footballer or rather leaving the sport due to other lifestyle choices. Although Donnelly and Young (1988, 226) refer to members' 'banishment from the group' when they do not perform key roles needed for acceptance by others within the sport subculture, this sense of banishment was not conveyed through the fieldwork or conversations with players. Rather, when players with salient selves moved away from this identification due to lifestyle choices their football self shifted across the Football Self Continuum to a more contingent position which accommodated their other activities more readily. It must be noted that a player has the mobility to shift their identity back and forth along the continuum in relation to lifestyle changes. Personally, my football self moved from salient at Lincoln Ladies to nearer the middle of the continuum during my university days and then back to extreme salience at WBA and finally towards contingent when playing more local football.

For a stable duration, the salient football self appeared constant for many of the players, this was also the case for me and my time with WBA. Football, for some of these players, was part of their character and personalities; it was viewed as deeply ingrained, almost biological. As Esme (U15) described, 'football is part of me'. Parents also observed how football impacted upon their daughter's sense of identity. Josie explained that her daughter's attitude towards football was different to that of her sons, who just thought football was fun and enjoyable; as noted:

> Alysha is really really committed, she loves it, it's like part of her, it's who she is; she's a footballer.
> She just lives and breathes football.

The way in which football affected their daughters was not overlooked by other parents in the study; Jack explained that for Hannah (U11) 'it's her identity'. The concept of salient football selves was not a hidden and secretive identity but was visible to others who noticed and understood the player to be a footballer. For example, players who showed a strong connection and engagement with football became known as 'the footballer in the family', and football was the source of topic for family gatherings and social occasions. Sometimes the label could be problematic, however:

> It's my identity. Sometimes it frustrates me because that's all people see me for. Like when we go to family parties that's all anyone ever talks about actually, I'm like there's a person behind the football.
>
> (Sarah)

This is a complex statement as initially Sarah admits football is her identity but later explains it's not all there is to her, she is 'behind the football'. The challenges to operating a salient football self were evident with Sarah whose football identity was so strong it had obscured her 'true' identity, the one 'behind' the football. As she stated, 'the thought of retiring scares the absolute living daylights out of me because I've never done anything else'. The incongruity Sarah described between her football self and her life stage (potential retirement) can be conceptualised through the interruption of her identity cycle, the 'broken loop' as referenced by Burke and Stets (2009, 77). By retiring Sarah's normal identity process and the way in which she organised her salient self would be interrupted, the way in which people currently recognised her pivoted on her football participation. My interpretation of this 'broken loop' is a shift away from the salient football self on the Football Self Continuum towards the contingent football self. A shift, potentially catalysed by a life stage change, from a salient football self towards that of a more contingent football self caused distress to players. These life stages could be retirement from the professional game, starting a family, moving jobs or going to university. This finding in particular may have implications for understanding how professional footballers cope with retirement and life after football. The reverse of this movement, for example a player with a contingent football self increasing their connection with the sport towards a more salient football self did not appear to generate the same issues.

Football identity to other players was not always viewed in the same way as Sarah:

> It's not who I am, I think it's part of who I am, and a big part. I think when sport defines who you are and that's all you think you are, that's not a good thing.
>
> (Ellie)

Ellie described the predicament Sarah faced when contemplating retirement: if football consumed one's entire life it was difficult to face life without it. This was interesting from Ellie who could be described as having a salient football self, and yet she did not let it define her. She admitted 'I have never lived without playing football' but that did not equate to not having any other aspirations outside of football. Even for the footballers with a salient football self, the usefulness of a continuum to understand the football self was important. The way players defined themselves varied along the continuum but it must be emphasised that the intricacies of negotiating the football self were personal. The breadth of my findings did allow for the general theorisations of contingent and salient selves to be made; however, the personal journey that footballers travelled was often nuanced with their own experiences and understanding of self.

The players who demonstrated salient football selves reported that football was expected to be a long-term part of their lives, and they hoped to have a career in and/or around football. The majority of club-level players wanted to excel in football and play at the highest level possible, including having international aspirations. Players from the youngest age category to the oldest discussed their desire to continue to play football and eventually play for England. According to her father, Olive (U13) viewed football participation as a credible career path and sought to play for England in the future. Ellie planned to move to Spain and dreamt of playing against Barcelona. Both Maisy (U17) and Miley (U15) explained the sacrifices they had made for football in relation to socialising with friends and family. For the majority of club players in this study, the football identity 'encompassed' them as individuals and connected to their present and perceived future lives through career choices. The way in which the players accommodated their enjoyment and passion for the game alongside challenges to participation will be explored in the next section.

The Sanctuary Paradox

This section, in particular, draws upon material used in my previous article and will be discussed and extended here.[3] All players involved in this study 'loved' to play football and enjoyed the game on many different levels and for various reasons. Many girls were introduced to the game by male coaches and Physical Education (PE) teachers, fathers and male friends recreationally, a finding consistent with previous research (e.g., Scraton et al., 1999; Stirling and Schulz, 2011). The players were aware of the traditional, societal views that football is a male sport to be played in masculine ways (Drury, 2011). Olive (U13) admitted 'I play boy sports' when describing the activities she enjoyed, and Gail (U15) explained that others were shocked when they discovered she played football, which they perceived as 'more of a guy's game'.

> Even though most people think it's like boy's play football, girls do ballet or whatever; when girls do play football I think they find it a bit more interesting and when they do watch it they find it a bit more surprising how good some girls can be.
>
> (Emma, School U13)

Emma described the surprise element connected with seeing talented female footballers. Players were aware of the 'sporting male hegemony' for which football is renowned (Renold, 2005, 57). The girls' and women's enjoyment of football ranged from 'the buzz you get from kicking that little bag of air about' (Jenny) to the chance to be competitive, socialise, get fit or consolidate an existing identity: football was meaningful. These reasons were in line with Grundlingh's (2010) findings; the women and girls in my research played because they were passionate about football and enjoyed the agency they could assert through their participation. It was the sense of freedom players felt through participation which was sacred to the women who played, and it allowed players to 'let go of gender role expectations' through participation (Grundlingh, 2010, 52).

It was clear that the girls and women significantly valued football. They relished the game itself, they enjoyed seeing their friends at training and they prized the feeling of escape and freedom they gained through playing. The players however did not enjoy the persistent bullying, teasing and berating for being girls and women who played football. Women players recalled being described as a 'man' and lesbian, whereas younger girls told stories of proving the boys wrong on the pitch and defying assumptions based on their appearance.

> **Lindsey**: My team's all of boys but they appreciate me playing because they think I'm good.
> **HP**: What does that make you feel like then?
> **Lindsey**: Happy
> **HP**: Does it?

Lindsey: Because they think I'm good.

HP: And would you rather boys think you're good or girls think you're good?

Lindsey: Rather boys because girls usually think everybody, every girl's good, but the boys always think every boy is good.

HP: So do you think you have to prove yourself more then to be good?

Lindsey: Yeah.

In this exchange, Lindsey (U9) explains the importance of boys' opinions and the meaning that has for your own football ranking and status. These findings are congruous with Caudwell's research on gender, sexuality and football which highlights the term 'butch' being used against players in a derogatory fashion and the struggle women and girls faced due to 'gendered stereotypes' (Caudwell, 2011, 333).

My own experiences of participating in football over the decades have involved instances of sexism, stereotyping and general misjudgement. The following memory snippet highlights the indirect 'othering' that is involved in being a woman footballer, a recollection from adulthood:

I was part of a team for a 'mixed' five-a-side football tournament in which I was either the only woman or one of two playing across the entire set-up. I was on the pitch warming-up with my all male teammates, when, just prior to kick off one of the opposition team members asked: 'would you like us to play with four rather than five players because we don't have any women?' A strange request and one which we accepted. Thinking back now, I am not sure why we accepted the request. Potentially because this would provide a winning advantage based purely on numbers and maybe because it would be amusing to see how the team reacted once the game kicked off. I hadn't even disguised my footballing heritage in the build-up to the game, fully kitted out in my old West Bromwich Albion training gear.

Anyway, straight from kick-off, a teammate passed me the ball to which I manoeuvred quickly onto my favoured right foot to swiftly pull off a shot which rocketed hard and low straight past the opposition's keeper. 1-0. At which point the opposition politely asked whether they could, on second thoughts, play as a team of five.

Now this memory is not one of bullying, it didn't upset me or bring me to tears, I wasn't heartbroken on the journey home or even felt a sense of injustice (more bemusement). But this is exactly why I am sharing it with you now. It is these indirect, seemingly empty experiences of sexism and discrimination that continue to shape and scaffold the way in which girls' and women's footballing journeys develop. This experience would not fuel the Football Association (FA) to start a campaign for justice or to encourage them to invest more resources into the game, nor would it catalyse FIFA to investigate inequality globally. But actually these experiences have significance; they unquestioningly form the basis for our cultural perceptions of women and football. It is these indirect and seemingly meaningless experiences that continue to crystallise women's participation in football as different, other and weak based on nothing more than appearance and stereotypes. All I wanted to do was to play a few games in a small-sided football competition, not have to accommodate rule changes implemented by others based on mythical ideas about my competencies as a woman player. Football is never just about football.

The majority of girls and women researched had directly experienced or were aware of gender-based football abuse: 'banter' or bullying that was linked to girls' and women's football. Kay (U15) referred to it as banter as though it was an expected, light-hearted and a *jokey* part of playing. Sarah, an experienced international footballer, spoke about being called a 'man' at school by the boys and yet highlighted that football provided a sanctuary for her:

> It wasn't just a hobby it was a bit of a sanctuary for me. It was somewhere where I went where I kinda felt safe and I felt like I was good at something, I felt like you could just forget everything else that was going on once you're playing.
>
> (Sarah)

This quote underlines my creation of the *Sanctuary Paradox*, namely the notion that girls and women accepted football abuse would be part of their lives but still found football to be a safe place to escape to and enjoy (see, Pielichaty, 2020). Parallels between this and the study of Israeli players by Parets et al. (2011) can be made here, in that players acknowledged the marginalisation of their game but still enjoyed the *safe bubble* in which they played. A departure from the study by Parets and others is that many of the players I worked with did not perceive football to be a hobby; football instead occupied a much more significant space in the lives of those with salient football selves. Current players did not therefore consolidate the marginal position of women's football by treating it as a hobby.

The epitome of the paradox was heightened by the harsh, cruel and undignified bullying received by players, adjacent with the peaceful and calming notion of a football sanctuary. Sarah explained the sanctuary as a safe space, where she excelled at something and would forget about the daily stresses of life. Yet ultimately, football playing was one of the causes of those daily stresses, whereby players' femininity and sexuality were being interrogated through playing. Femininity, for these players, was questioned on the basis of the perceived female athlete paradox (Kassing, 2018) which continued to perpetuate across the football sites examined. Also, the players' sexual identities in relation to the lesbian label often attached to the game (Stirling and Schulz, 2011) were also shown to be a source of teasing in the current study.

Amy's football sanctuary related to stress relief which commensurate with the idea of football as a safe place or retreat:

> I love football because it's something I've wanted to do all my life, I get to see my mates, it's a good way to relieve problems/stress of school and I get to do something I love.
>
> (Amy, U15)

In this context Amy mentioned problems at school which connected the importance and significance of both football playing and school life. The use of space and place here can be taken to be both physically and socially constructed space where girls and women would *go to* when playing football. Peter explained that his daughter had mild dyslexia but football came naturally to her and was her 'release' and a dimension of her life she could achieve in; 'it's somewhere she can go and can excel'. The football sanctuary for Olive was a space in which she was confident and able to release any anxieties or stresses potentially linked to her dyslexia. Football in the following example provided a safe place devoid of judgement and a catalyst for freedom:

> When you want to play football you just kind of feel like a different person, all the things that everybody said about you just kind of like goes away. You are just kind of in the moment on how it is. Like you forget about what anyone's ever said to you,

what anyone's ever like judged, it's just you on your own with a football.

(Emma, U13)

Furthermore, the concept of sanctuary is relevant to all ages of footballers:

> Because now I've got two children and kinda life's so hectic it is just nice to get away from that and obviously it is something to do which I love and obviously being back with the girls I used to play with it is so nice to build that relationship and become friends again.

(Michelle)

Michelle discussed her return to football and how it offered her a personal space of freedom. It was not only the players that football became a sanctuary for but also the parents involved in their daughter's football playing. Football for these parents was a safe space for them to engage with and socialise with others, the paradoxical aspect was omitted for parents because they did not report having received direct abuse for having football playing daughters. The concept of sanctuary became particularly evident for one mother, Hazel who became a pioneer for the girls' and women's game once her daughter started playing and was involved in the organisation and administration of a local club. During this time, Hazel became extremely ill and acknowledged football as a 'therapy' for her at this point:

> Yeah I can forget about everything else that's going on and just get involved with this piece of paperwork or make these few phone calls and deal with something else that's been different and taken me out of where I was.

(Hazel)

By being involved in her daughter's football participation, football indirectly provided Hazel with a sanctuary away from her illness, removing her physically and emotionally from a difficult situation with her health. The word 'forget' is used by Emma, Hazel and Sarah to indicate the way football involvement provided not only a physical space but an emotional space away from their everyday strains. Kassing (2018, 1098) acknowledges that paradoxes 'can be empowering' which is the case for the players here, who viewed the sanctuary aspect of participation as liberating. Girls and women managed the Sanctuary Paradox by normalising the negativity they may have received from others for playing football, whether by side-lining it as 'banter' like Katie, or by 'proving the boys wrong' through skilful play like eight-year-old Lindsey. It must be noted that although the Sanctuary Paradox related to many of the girls and women involved in the research it did not cover all of their experiences.

Conclusion

As discussed in this chapter, the relationship between football and player is complicated, personal and fluid. Players with salient football selves are dedicated and committed to football for a time-limited period, whereby their identities hinge on the existence of football and their relationship with it. Players with contingent football selves enjoy football in a more recreational sense, negotiating their football self in relation to changing contexts and social activities. All players express a joy for football. This book offers fresh insight into the experiences of girls and women footballers as few previous studies have offered extensive theorisation around the meaning of football to girls and women players. A love for the game does involve an acceptance of gender-based bullying and social stigma which continues to mar the enjoyment of the game. The following chapter will examine the cultural and ideological challenges to girls' and women's football in relation to gender appropriateness and expectations.

Notes

1 This chapter is derived in part from an article published in *Qualitative Journal of Sport, Exercise and Health* published online on 26.11.18 copyright Taylor & Francis, available online: https://www.tandfonline.com/doi/abs/10.1080/2159676X.2018.1549094?journalCode=rqrs21.
2 This chapter is also derived in part from the following article: Pielichaty, H, Pleasure and the Sanctuary Paradox: Experiences of Girls and Women Playing Soccer, International Review for the Sociology of Sport (55/6) pp. 788–806. Copyright © [2020] (Sage). doi:10.1177/1012690219857023.
3 Pielichaty, H, Pleasure and the Sanctuary Paradox: Experiences of Girls and Women Playing Soccer, International Review for the Sociology of Sport (55/6) pp. 788–806. Copyright © [2020] (Sage). doi:10.1177/1012690219857023.

References

Allen-Collinson, J. and Brown, R. (2012) I'm a Reddie and a Christian! Identity negotiations amongst first-year university students. *Studies in Higher Education*, 37(4), 497–511.

Allen-Collinson, J. and Hockey, J. (2007) 'Working out' identity: distance runners and the management of disrupted identity. *Leisure Studies*, 26(4), 381–398.

Bettis, P.J. and Adams, N.G. (eds.) (2005) *Geographies of girlhood: identities in-between.* Mahwah: Lawrence Erlbaum Associates Publishers.

Burke, P.J. and Stets, J.E. (2009) *Identity theory.* Oxford: Oxford University Press.

Caudwell, J. (2011) Gender, feminism and football studies. *Soccer and Society*, 12(3), 330–344.

Cooper, F. (2005) *Colonialism in Question: theory, knowledge, history.* London: University of California Press.

Curry, C. (1998) Adolescence. In: Trew, K. and Kremer, J. (eds.) *Gender and psychology.* London: Arnold, 107–113.

Donnelly, P. and Young, K. (1988) The construction and confirmation of identity in sport subcultures. *Sociology of Sport Journal*, 5(3), 223–240.

Drury, S. (2011) 'It seems really inclusive in some ways, but…inclusive just for people who identify as lesbian': discourses of gender and sexuality in a lesbian-identified football club. *Soccer and Society*, 12(13), 421–442.

Gledhill, A. and Harwood, C. (2015) A holistic perspective on career development in UK female soccer players: a negative case analysis. *Psychology of Sport and Exercise*, 21, 65–77.

Grundlingh, M. (2010) Boobs and balls: exploring issues of gender and identity among women soccer players at Stellenbosch University. *Agenda: Empowering Women for Gender*, 24(85), 45–53.

Harris, J. (2007) Doing gender on and off the pitch: the world of female football players. *Sociological Research Online*, 12(1). Available from: http://www.socresonline.org.uk/12/1/harris.html [Accessed 5 March 2015].

Jeanes, R. (2005) Girls, football participation and gender identity. In: Bramham, P. and Caudwell, J. (eds.) *Sport, Active Leisure and Youth Cultures.* Eastbourne: LSA, 75–96.

Jeanes, R. (2011) 'I'm into high heels and make up but I still love football': exploring identity and football participation with preadolescent girls. *Soccer and Society*, 12(3), 402–420.

Kassing, J.W. (2018) Confronting the female athlete paradox with humor and irony: a thematic analysis of SoccerGrlProbs YouTube video content. *Sport in Society*, 21(7), 1096–1111.

Lester, J. (2004) Spirit, identity, and self in mountaineering. *Journal of Humanistic Psychology*, 44(1), 86–100.

Oxenham, G. (2017) *Under the lights and in the dark: untold stories of women's soccer.* London: Icon Books.

Parets, S., Levy M. and Galily, Y. (2011) National and gender identity perceptions among female football players in Israel. *Soccer and Society*, 12(2), 228–248.

Pielichaty, H. (2015) 'It's like equality now; it's not as if it's the old days': an investigation into gender identity development and football participation of adolescent girls. *Soccer and Society*, 16(4), 493–507.

Pielichaty, H. (2019) Identity salience and the football self: a critical ethnographic study of women and girls in football. *Qualitative Research in Sport, Exercise and Health*, 11(4), 527–542.

Pielichaty, H. (2020) Pleasure and the sanctuary paradox: Experiences of girls and women playing soccer. *International Review for the Sociology of Sport*, 55(6), 788–806.

Renold, E. (2005) *Girls, boys and junior sexualities: exploring children's gender and sexual relations in the primary school*. London: Routledge Falmer.

Scraton, S., Fasting, K., Pfister, G. and Brunel, A. (1999) It's still a man's game? The experiences of top-level European women footballers. *International Review for the Sociology of Sport*, 34(2), 99–111.

Sprague, J. (2016) *Feminist methodologies for critical researchers: bridging differences*, 2nd edition. Lanham: Rowman and Littlefield.

Stebbins, R.A. (2008) *Serious leisure*. London: Transaction Publishers.

Stirling, L. and Schulz, J. (2011) Women's football: still in the hands of men. *Sport Management International Journal*, 7(2), 53–78.

Stone, C. (2007) The role of football in everyday life. *Soccer and Society*, 8(2/3), 169–184.

Stryker, S. (1968) Identity salience and role performance: the relevance of symbolic interaction theory for family research. *Journal of Marriage and Family*, 30(4), 558–564.

Valentine, G. (1997) 'My son's a bit dizzy', 'my wife's a bit soft': gender, children and cultures of parenting. *Gender, Place and Culture*, 4(1), 37–62.

Wagg, S., Brick, C., Wheaton, B. and Caudwell. J. (2009) *Key concepts in sports studies*. London: Sage Publications.

Wyn, J., Lantz, S. and Harris, A. (2011) Beyond the 'transitions' metaphor: family relations and young people in late modernity. *Journal of Sociology*, 48(1), 3–22.

4 Gender and the binary evolution

In June 2019 *The New York Times* wrote a piece entitled: *World Cup Players Say Muscles and Makeup Mix Just Fine, Thanks* and the article remarked on the perceived incongruity between athletic prowess and femininity (McCann, 2019), which brings us to the focus of this chapter. There remain cultural and ideological challenges to girls and women who choose to play football, and these often manifest through the visual re/presentation of bodies and beauty. As Hargreaves (2000, 3) points out:

> Gendered heroism is being constantly challenged by women who are appropriating the narratives of maleness and transforming themselves from victims into superstars.

The FIFA World Cup in 2019 certainly seemed like a space for footballers to exaggerate their femininities whilst performing the traditionally masculine act of playing. Players stood over free-kicks with bright red lipstick aglow; others weaved through defensive lines leaving only a flash of exotic hair colour in their wake. This was the year that femininity seemed to pacify all previous connotations of *butch tomboy* footballers that weighed heavily on the women's game. Surely, a cultural change wasn't that simple? The empirical data that I draw upon within this chapter provides a more complex picture of the relationship between player, appearance and football. It is first important to outline the general but key discussions connected to gender identities in football before moving on to more detail surrounding bodies, beauty and sexualities. The final section of this chapter examines authenticity, credibility and negotiating the contemporary female footballer visual.

Gender identities and football participation

Childhood and school experiences of gender, often tied to the 'perceived' gender binary, influence the way gender identities are constructed and developed. Howard and Hollander (1997) explain that people tend to view their gender identity as either male or female in dichotomous terms. Individual gender identities can be formulated and defined by abiding by the limits of the two gender categories (Parets et al., 2011), which is often easier than deviating from them, which can result in harassment (Renold, 2005). As a result, girls still feel pressure to conform to hyper-feminine and heterosexual girly girl identities (Allan, 2009) and boys believe male bodies should be strong and masculine (Drummond, 2012).

When women enter the male-dominated world of football, they need to challenge the assumptions relating to *real* women's sport (Brus and Trangbæk, 2004). Women's football has been criticised for being an 'inferior copy' (Hjelm, 2011, 143) of men's football, and sitting 'outside' of what football is perceived to be by the masses (Dunn and Welford, 2015, 91). This social positioning means that not only the performance of the women's game is monitored but so is the way it 'appears', looks and presents itself. Women footballers are subjected to criticism about defying socially accepted female values and masculinising themselves (Hallmann, 2012). This 'masculinising process' is arguably being challenged by contemporary footballers, as outlined in the introduction, but to what extent does the presentation of football on the world stage translate to other levels of participation?

These cultural attitudes, so deeply rooted in women's football, present barriers to participation which are very difficult to combat; it has been argued that girls need to distance themselves from traditional femininity to be accepted into the footballing world (Stirling and Schulz, 2011). This was also the case in the research by Scraton et al. (1999) where female footballers removed themselves from the ideal of feminine and female and embraced their tomboy persona as a positive element of their identity. The footballers in Cox and Thompson's (2000) study who defined themselves as tomboys did so on the basis of their behaviour (climbing trees, being competitive), appearance (looking like boys and not wearing dresses) and being physically active. In Jeanes' study, girls would play football only if it did not 'compromise their projection of a visual feminine identity' (Jeanes, 2011, 411).

Despite the connection between football and masculinities, the girls in Jeanes' (2005) study did not seem to have too many troubles with balancing their playing with their chosen gender identity. The 'girlie girls' did not find playing football inhibiting, and their football identity was placed alongside the other identities between which they moved (contingent selves). For the tomboy girls, playing football reinforced their chosen gender identity, which involved disregarding the typical normative mould of femininity. The players in Cox and Thompson's (2000) study did not perceive the tomboy label as negative but rather a reassuring way to explain their gendered self.

Other research demonstrates the fluidity of gender identities in connection with girl and women players:

> The identities of Maties [players from Stellenbosch University] women soccer players can be considered as a continuous process, formed by their subjective experiences as women soccer players and therefore gendered. Their identity is neither single or fixed, but a process constructed within power relations.
>
> (Grundlingh, 2010, 48)

This fluidity, however, can sometimes be stunted; the girls in Jeanes' (2005, 92) research were concerned about playing football in the future, when gender would 'no longer [be] open for negotiation', as sacrifices would have to made with regard to conformity to more conventional female roles.

Bodies and women's football

The relationship between image and women's football becomes even more complex when considering the women's body.

> Women must look like women – especially if they are involved in activities which have been established as 'male' i.e. football. If women fail to look like women then they are read as abject.
>
> (Caudwell, 2000, 107)

> Prescribed ideals for what girls and women should look like and how they should behave in the public space, cautiously, moderately and without ostentatious body behaviour, complicate their way of playing football and make it more difficult.
>
> (Hjelm, 2011, 156)

There are also certain signifiers of the body that are used to convey typically feminine or masculine characteristics, such as the length of hair, type of clothes worn, jewellery and decoration and the use of cosmetics. It must be noted that:

> Sport and active leisure clearly have an overwhelming regulatory influence on femininity and masculinity and gendered body motif.
>
> (Caudwell, 2000, 99)

Hair is a significant symbol of femininity, and the ponytail for football women is seen to signify femaleness and heterosexuality (Cox and Thompson, 2000). Furthermore, women's football does not escape the societal pressures placed on women and their bodies to strive for perfection, 'fatness is observed and evaluated' on the football pitch as a means of assessing capability and talent (Cox and Thompson, 2000, 13). More recently, an examination of professional women footballers reported a toxic culture of obsession surrounding weight and body image (Tomas, 2020).

Caudwell acknowledges that the term '*butch* is used to belittle and devalue women and their achievements' within the sporting environment (Caudwell, 2003, 377). In a later study, Caudwell also explains that the butch typology for some players becomes central to the understanding of authenticity and consolidation of female masculinity (Caudwell, 2007). Consequentially, hyper-femininity may also be produced by women players in response to the masculine image of the game (Scraton et al., 1999). Accommodating a feminine image, however, within a sporting setting can be viewed as being 'unsportsmanlike' (Scully, 1998, 209), because portraying a feminine identity does not align to sporting success. It seems then that girls and women playing sports occupy a difficult position, a complex space of skewed norms and unreachable acceptance.

Empirical data: football and gender identities

Girls and women were acutely aware that football was deemed a traditionally masculine sport and as a result acknowledged the connectivity between football playing and tomboyism. The majority of players rejected this connection to tomboy status due to their disengagement with the football girl and tomboy stereotype. The players did not occupy one fixed gendered position but rather operated across a wider spectrum of gender possibilities. Players were not limited to tomboy status by playing football but *gender blended* through wearing make-up, socialising with friends and playing football amongst other sports. Findings indicated that players' gender operated in fluid and complex ways commensurate to the kaleidoscopic patterns alive to them in the form of context and environment (cf. Spade and Valentine, 2017). There were times when players conformed to practices of traditional femininity such as wearing dresses for special occasions, socialising and going out with friends; and then other times when they did not, such as when playing football. Alice (U13) explained that she felt peoples' assumptions of football tomboys were unfounded, and that football girls could also enjoy stereotypically feminine activities. Alice discussed the fact she liked football, rugby, make-up and wearing fake nails, 'I see it as people say you can either be a girlie girl or a tomboy but you can't be in-between'. The players were aware of the apparent gender binary of male/masculine and female/feminine (see Corbett, 2009) but did not themselves operate in binary terms.

During parental discussions surrounding gender, Steve and Jack reported:

HP: What is it like being a dad of a female footballer? What is it like?

Steve: She's a boy really, she's a tomboy.

Jack: So is mine.

Steve: So she doesn't wear any girl's clothes, she hasn't got any girl's clothes whatsoever.

Jack: No.

Steve: She doesn't do any girlie things.

Jack: Hannah's the same.

Steve: Nothing whatsoever. Just like having a boy really.

HP: Has she always been like that?

Steve: Yes.

Jack: Hannah has, Hannah's got an older brother, six years older so she's always looked up to him.

Another dad, explained his daughter, Sian used to call herself Josh when she was younger because she liked doing *boy things*. Players, although they themselves demonstrated fluid identities, often connected femininity with image and attire and masculinity with behaviour and activity. Despite this fluidity, the tomboy and girlie girl descriptors were significant to the players in the current study.

Clare (U13) was perceived to be a girlie girl as described by my own observation:

Clare complains about her eyes hurting and is opening them up very wide and other girls tell her she looks as though she's about to cry. Clare responds 'my mascara is going to run and that's worse!' The coach reacts in disbelief and questions why she is wearing mascara.

This illustrated Clare's position in the group as a girlie girl, a category of girl that she reinforced consistently during football training sessions. During a pair discussion between Clare and Becky (U13s), Clare was not so clear about her distinctive girlie girl character:

HP: What type of girl do you think you are? If you had to think of anything...

Clare: Maybe like, a bit of both because when, like, people from here know there's a big occasion and we'll get in a dress and some heels but when I'm playing football I would be like a kind of like tomboy.

HP: So when you say a bit of both, what are the both then you mean?

Clare: Like girlie girl and tomboy.

HP: Yes, so do you think you can be both and play football as well?

Clare: Yes.

HP: What about yourself? [asks Becky]

Becky: Well I'm not really a girlie girl, I don't really get dressed up in dresses or anything. In football I'm probably more of a tomboy but I'm not like, I'm not like a girlie girl.

Both girls showed an awareness of the perceived binary notion of girlhood, the first option being that of girlie and the second option of tomboy. Clare did not confine herself to the girlie girl option and instead explained she was 'a bit of both' and could act in both girlie and non-girlie ways which were demonstrated through appearance for girlie-ness and behaviour for tomboy-ness. Becky noted she was not a girlie girl or a tomboy and used the word 'probably' to portray the lack of terminology available to her in order to describe her own gendered self.

Girls demonstrated fluid identities to allow them to experience and enjoy both typically feminine and masculine activities. During a conversation with Tiffany (U13), this discussion around gender identity acquired a new dimension:

HP: Do you think any type of girl can play football?

Tiffany: No. Coz I think a girlie girlie girl like is into shopping and all that rubbish.

HP: So, a girlie girl is into shopping and all that rubbish?
Tiffany: Yeah.
HP: And she wouldn't be very good at football?
Tiffany: No.
HP: Why do you have to be a different type of girl to play football do you think?
Tiffany: You have to be sporty and like and you have to like enjoy doing sports and like in PE you don't like say *oh it's PE* like you've got to love PE and everything.
HP: So you have to have it close to who you are?
Tiffany: Yeah.
HP: Do you think any of your teammates are girlie girls?
Tiffany: Clare.
HP: Is she?
Tiffany: Yeah.
HP: So Clare's a girlie girl and plays football?
Tiffany: Yeah but she's not like the most girliest girl like, she's... she's just Clare.

For Tiffany, being a footballer was an important role and to qualify for this role a girl must demonstrate a love of sport and in particular must thoroughly enjoy Physical Education (PE). Tiffany was dismissive of girls who did not share her commitment and passion for PE and regarded girlie girls as being too busy shopping for clothes to be interested in football. Traditionally, football has been perceived as a masculine sport exclusive to men and boys (Harris, 2007) and now, according to Tiffany, to men, boys and sporty girls who 'do not like shopping'. When questioned about her teammate, Clare, Tiffany's views of the two fixed states of gender changed rapidly. Clare was deemed to be an exception to the rule because her girlie-ness was not extreme, she explained Clare is not 'the most girliest' of girls and rather perceived her as an isolated case, 'she's just Clare' not located within a girlie girl homogenous group.

Younger girls at the academy also demonstrated complexities when describing their gender in relation to football participation, as the U9 group expressed:

HP: What kind of girl are you?
Harriet: A tomboy.
HP: How come?
Harriet: Because I play with Power Rangers, Black Ops and like zombies.

Charlotte: Tomboy.
HP: Why are you a tomboy?
Charlotte: Because I play football.
Lindsey: I'm pretty in pink.
HP: What do you mean?
Lindsey: I'm girlie and like doing my hair.
HP: Can you be both girlie and play football?
Lindsey: Erm.
Harriet: She's a tombirl.
HP: What's that?
Harriet: When you're a tomboy girl.
Lindsey: I like fighting with my brothers.

Unlike players in the U13 group, younger girls were very forward about being categorised as a tomboy: a definition for these players that consolidated their status as footballer. The phrase 'tomboy' was potentially straightforward for the players but their understanding of gender was not. These players were inventive with their approach to gender understanding and attempted to find better ways to describe who they were. Harriet defined her tomboy character in connection with enjoying typically masculine toys and liking gruesome creatures such as zombies. Charlotte simply stated she was a tomboy because she played football; it was a very simple equation for her. Lindsey enjoyed doing her hair, associating beauty and appearance with typically feminine signifiers of girlie girl. When Lindsey struggled to process the relationship between girlie girl and footballer, Harriet offered her a solution in the form of 'tombirl'. The tombirl identity, through further discussions with Harriet, was something that she had heard about at school and related, in her words, to girls who 'wear dresses and like zombies'. Harriet also used the concept of 'tomgoy', which seemed synonymous with tombirl.

It must be noted that the majority of players used the phrase 'tomboy' or 'girlie girl' without prompt which implied the phrases remained heavily ingrained in contemporary girlhood discourse. A similar suggestion appeared in the school group discussions (U13), whereby the girls presented the phrase tomgirl to describe a girl who shared characteristics of both a tomboy and a girlie girl. Rebecca stated, 'I wouldn't say I'm a girlie girl but I wouldn't say I'm a tomboy', the traditional gender dichotomy for some girls was just not workable. It is very clear that girls are searching for creative means to define their gendered selves as the notion of a straightforward tomboy or girlie girl was too restrictive, alien and unfamiliar.

Lisa (U15) described herself as 'very tomboy' and her football participation neatly tied in with this understanding of herself. This was more difficult to define for some girls, however:

> I hate it when people call you tomboy because just because you play sport doesn't mean you're a tomboy. You don't walk around wearing boy's clothes, you don't act like a boy but you just like to do sports that any other person can play.
>
> (Sophie School U13)

Sophie was frustrated by the assumption that being sporty equated with being a tomboy; she later described herself as a girlie girl who liked to play sports. Instead of the notion of girlie girl being equated with dresses and shopping Sophie instead connected it to sports participation.

Older girls Miley (U15) and Maise (U17) described their team as a 'mixture' of girls, and both believed that any type of girl could play football. Alysha (U17) stated that: 'I'm quite girlie girl outside of football', which perhaps indicated her sense of identity movement in relation to being a footballer and being girlie. Zoe (U17) described herself as both sporty and girlie in that she liked wearing dresses and make-up outside of participating in sport. Zoe reported that her sister Kay (U15) used to be a tomboy but more recently 'transitioned' to girlie girl due to the extensive make-up she wore to school. Kay found it easy to juggle football playing with being a girlie girl and enjoyed dressing up and going out at the weekend with her school friends. Poppy (U15) said that 'I can be me and still play football as well' in response to being girlie and wearing make-up too. For Poppy, who was also a club-level footballer, football was one of the things she loved to do as well as being girlie and experimenting with femininity. This link between femininity and appearance (make-up, hair and body image) was not as easy to manage and understand for some girls in the study.

'If they're caked in make-up I just laugh'

Make-up provided a substantial talking point for the girls and young women; the way in which the opposition team wore make-up was commented upon and judged. This initially appeared significant within the fieldwork through conversation with Zoe (U17):

Zoe: I know this sounds really bad but like on some match days like you get there and you can see the ones who are going to be the better players, because they, I don't know they seem more focussed like. I don't know, you can kinda see by their looks as well, I know it sounds really bad.

HP: No, go on.

Zoe: Like you can see the ones which have loads of make-up on and their hair's all like straightened and stuff and you can sort of see they're not, they're clearly not, like you could get it completely wrong, do you know what I mean but on a match day that's sort of what I generally tend to think and look at and think. That's the first thing I notice in the other team, notice the people who have all the make-up on, have their hair all back.

Miley (U15) shared similar sentiments: 'if they're caked in make-up I just laugh', whereas Maisy (U17) questioned the time the opposition player must have spent applying their make-up rather than practising their football skills. During their pair interview Miley and Maisy joked that if an opposition player had a 'massive orange face' then they would stand out and get noticed, but not necessarily for the right reasons. The girls admitted that sometimes the heavily made-up girls did play better than they had expected. This also resonates with Russell's (2004, 566) research which highlighted the contradiction between the 'performing body' and 'social body' of sportswomen. In a sense the opposition players wearing make-up could be described as displaying their social bodies on the football pitch, a space more suitable for performing bodies only. Miley and Maisy made judgements based on other players' appearance prior to seeing them kick a ball because the normative understanding of girlie girl (as expressed through make-up wearing) is linked to being weak and inept at sport. It is at this point I recall the memory I share in the previous chapter about being ability-judged by the opposition men's five aside team before kicking a ball – is there any difference here? We must remember that both males and females subject one another to gender-based stereotypes.

The display of femininity through make-up wearing needed to be carefully balanced to not exceed the 'correct' amount. It was not just the older girls in the study who were affected by the application and non-application of make-up. Harriet (U9), a self-confessed tomboy, still wore make-up, when asked why she used blusher, she replied 'to make my skin look nice'. Harriet balanced her tomboy identity and fondness for cosmetics in a very fluid fashion. This amused the other girls who mocked Harriet about this and found the act of wearing make-up funny. Clare (U13) during one training session claimed, 'my moisturiser has dried into my skin', a comment which reflected Clare's girlie girl persona as demonstrated by her actions and statements throughout the study. A minority of girls in each age group at the academy used make-up for a multitude of expressed reasons; however, for other players make-up was deemed impractical and symbolised low footballing ability and a lack of professionalism.

Femininity and clothing

Other aspects of appearance, such as clothing, were viewed as more fluid and changeable by the players. Players negotiated their gender fluidity through the compartmentalisation of their clothing. Clothing is an important feature of gender, and Holland and Harpin (2015, 296) explained that tomboys felt 'physically freer' by their clothing choices and wearing skirts and dresses was highly contentious. Most players did not locate themselves within the extreme dichotomy definition of tomboy or girlie girl. Gender fluidity was often managed by the way clothing was compartmentalised to match their chosen activity and identity for that particular context. Lucy and Kelly's (U13) conversation helps to explain this:

HP: If you were to describe yourself, what type of girl would you say you are? There is no right or wrong answer but what words would you use to describe yourself?
Kelly: Girlie-ish.
Lucy: Yeah I have girlie clothes but then I just play football and just have football clothes. Like I have really girlie clothes hanging up in my wardrobe and then at the bottom I have got all my football kit and that. So if I want to go to the park or something and play football I just go to the bottom of my wardrobe and get joggers out of there. But I have quite a lot of girlie clothes and I go out in town with my friends a lot so, girlie-ish, but I do like to play football and get in joggers and get dirty.
HP: So do you think you can be girlie and play football?
Both: Yes.
HP: So do you think actually to be girlie you can just play football anyway and it maybe isn't a tomboy thing anymore, what do you reckon?
Lucy: Sometimes people refer to it as being tomboyish but I think, looking at me and all of my other friends they have lots of girlie clothes and then play football so I don't think it's tomboyish.

HP: What do you think Kelly?

Kelly: [Remains quiet].

Lucy: My friends used to scream when they got mud on their hands when we were training at primary school and I just said 'don't be pathetic, it's just mud' and then they started screaming, but most girls there were just like really girlie girls. My friend said I taught her to play football and I inspired her to play football, so she started to play football after that.

HP: How would you describe yourself Kelly?

Kelly: I have girlie clothes but then I've got a cupboard with all of my football stuff.

HP: So when I said what type of girl are you, you told me about clothes straight away, do you think clothes are what makes you a girlie girl or a tomboy then?

Kelly: Not necessarily.

Lucy: Because if you think about it girls like boys and really girlie girls will try to impress the boys but clothes sort of make a difference. Because if you walk around in your joggers all of the time, they're going to think you're a tomboy.

Kelly: A chav.

Lucy: Yeah a chav [both giggle].

HP: So do you think girlie girls want to find boyfriends basically?

Lucy: Yeah

Lucy: Like they're more into boys than what tomboys are.

Kelly: I wouldn't class myself as a tomboy because there's someone that lives where I live and they're a proper tomboy, like a boy.

Lucy: That's what I thought, there's a girl that lived down my street and she was a proper tomboy and I looked at her and then looked at myself and thought I'm not a tomboy at all. She like wore proper boy's clothes like my brother would wear.

In this lengthy exchange, both Kelly and Lucy drew upon a variety of discourses surrounding girlhood. First, both girls expressed an ease of transition between a girlie girl and a tomboy position which was demonstrated through wardrobe compartmentalisation. At the start of the exchange with Kelly and Lucy, both players agreed that any kind of girl could play football, but once the conversation was underway the limitations of the girlie girl construction came to the fore in the form of screaming about mud and spending too much time trying to get a boyfriend. Also, the football girls disconnected themselves from extreme versions of tomboy when describing and comparing themselves to 'proper' tomboys with 'proper' boys' clothes. When Kelly said she's 'girlie-ish', this was the only language she could locate to explain how she was not an extreme girlie girl ('like really girlie girls'), nor was she a 'proper' tomboy. Rather both players moved fluidly between multi-faceted kaleidoscopic patterns connected to football, school and home life which organically shifted to provide the variety of gender options within the kaleidoscope (see Spade and Valentine, 2008, 2017). The fluidity experienced by the players was still constrained by traditional norms linking football participation to tomboyism.

Janet, mother of twins Ellie and Suzie, explained that from the age of two years old both of her daughters 'hated wearing dresses' and from that point onwards she knew she would not be taking them to dance or gymnastics, as these were deemed activities stereotypically linked to femininity and girls' participation, whereas football was not. Janet grouped the act of dress wearing with typically feminine activities such as dancing and gymnastics, which is in line with a traditional feminine identity status. Similarly to the women in Caudwell's (2003) research, Sarah retrospectively described herself as a tomboy, 'I was always getting dirty, I was always scraping my knees, my hands'. This boisterous behaviour was often associated with tomboyism, and Sarah admitted 'I was pretty much one of the boys when I was growing up'. Similarly, Sabine also described herself as a tomboy when she was younger as she reminisced about playing sport and spending time with boys outdoors. Michelle, an older player, reflected on being a tomboy as a child and how all of her friends were also tomboys and explained that football 'fitted in easily' with this persona. Tomboyism, as experienced by these women, provided a space for 'freedom, mobility and physicality' (Holland and Harpin, 2015, 296) which was consolidated through football participation.

Appearance was also an issue addressed by Sophie during a school conversation:

> They'll look at you and think oh I never thought you'd be something like that [in reference to a footballer], I'd thought you'd be a person to go out wear dresses and be all glitter people.
>
> (School U13)

Sophie described the disjointedness between her reality and societal perceptions of girls who played football. Sophie explained that her girlie behaviour and personality confused some people when they learnt of her football playing because it did not mirror the expectations connected to gender and sport. She referred to 'glitter people' as girlie girls, those girls who like sparkle and glamour. The concept of *glitter girls* was analogous to the girlies/girlie girl category in previous research (Reay, 2001; Renold, 2005; Jeanes, 2011). Glitter people or glitter girls chose to wear dresses, which as discovered previously in this study epitomised the archetypical peak of extreme girlie-ness. Contrary to previous literature it was the wearing of dresses and not hair length or style (see Cox and Thompson, 2000; Knijnik and Horton, 2013) that appeared to be a significant indicator of normative femininity here.

Appearance, bodies and beauty

The footballers spent time discussing the themes of physical appearance and beauty. Esme (U15) reported that any type of girl could play football and she did not think anything of appearance. This was supported by U11 girls during a group conversation who explained that it was not necessary to look good to be a girl, although Fiona stated that her friends at school believed it was. The girls showed an understanding of different viewpoints and pressures from other individuals: an expressed interpretation of the differences between the 'physical [football] body' and the 'social body' (Russell, 2004), the players understood that the social environment influenced gendered perceptions.

Gender displays were changeable and dependent on environment and complex ideologies. Players selected and utilised different ways to 'do' gender at different times, such as wearing long eye-lashes to football training or to go out with friends at weekends. Similar to West and Zimmerman's (1987) ethnomethodological theorisation that gender is something we 'do' and have to produce, the players in this study did gender their own way, whether through playing football, seeing friends or having a manicure. Albeit, their 'own way' of doing gender was still influenced and impacted by complex ideology about the appropriateness of some forms of femininity in connection with football. The following image is my player photo from my time at West Bromwich Albion (WBA) Women and it looks nothing like my 'playing' self, I had chosen to put make-up on and wear my hair down, to present my 'social body' for the photo-shoot. This makes me laugh now, because the football identity demonstrated in this photo is not my 'true' football self, but rather a feminised representation of 'Hanya doing football' (Figure 4.1).

Figure 4.1 West Bromwich Albion Women FC circa 2009.

Empirical data indicated that footballers' talent was judged on physical appearance, which coheres with Caudwell's (2007) suggestion that it was the 'butch' archetypical women's footballer that symbolised authenticity. Authenticity is a strong term used here to demonstrate the deep-rooted connectivity between women's football and the putative butch image (Cox and Thompson, 2001): these two reference points have become synonymous with one another and therefore reify authenticity: what it is to be a 'proper' women's footballer. The 'butch' depiction of women footballers links participation to lesbianism and masculinity (Caudwell, 2003; Harris, 2005) and not to hetero-femininity. The symbolic status of make-up wearing promoted a hyper-feminine image which was viewed as inappropriate and questionable within the realm of football. The complexity of this deepens due to the common associations between femininity and womanhood in which women are pressured to be beautiful, slim and feminine (Bordo, 2003). Players were resentful towards 'butch' and lesbian discourse, and yet through observations and conversations were critical of players who formulated more feminine appearances.

Conclusion

The relationship between woman, body and beauty is socially imbued and complex, even more so against the masculinised backdrop of British football. Women and girl footballers are under pressure to look a certain way to play the sport; they are required to balance the gendered self of athletic, serious, thin and not heavily made up. Ultra-feminine displays threatened the seriousness of the women's game and were monitored and belittled by other players. As Scully states it seems that a feminine image within a sports setting is 'unsportsmanlike' (Scully, 1998, 209) which was reified by some players who linked feminine appearance with a lack of talent and respect for the game. Players scrutinised the appearance of other players to negotiate the two existing ideological stances: first, women and girls should be feminine, slim and beautiful, and second, to be good at sport you must act in masculine ways. These conflicting demands on women to be both sexy-normative and professional (Aapola et al., 2004) surfaced here. The conflict appears in relation to coupling professionalism and seriousness with an image of sexiness: an image traditionally connected to weakness and passivity. Women's professionalism was deeply dependent on the extent to which a sexy-normative appearance was effectively restrained and not overtly displayed.

Even though the majority of participants expressed that any type of girl could play football, on deeper investigation it appeared that self-confessed girlie girls, tomboys or 'mixtures' still had to negotiate the discourse and presuppositions linked to aspects of girlhood. It was acceptable, therefore, to be a footballer who expressed girlie girl characteristics as long as they did not compromise the physical act of playing. The gender performance of girlie girls on and off the field was critically examined and surveyed by other players. Critical examination continues in the next chapter but this time with a focus on football families and how girls and women players negotiate their love of the game with family connections and commitments.

References

Aapola, S., Gonick, M. and Harris, A. (2004) *Young femininity: girlhood, power and social change*. Basingstoke: Palgrave Macmillan.

Allan, A.J. (2009) The importance of being a 'lady': hyper-femininity and heterosexuality in the private, single-sex primary school. *Gender and Education*, 21(2), 145–158.

Bordo, S. (2003) *Unbearable weight: feminism, Western culture, and the body*, 10th edition. London: University of California Press.

Brus, A. and Trangbæk, E. (2004) Asserting the right to play – women's football in Denmark. In: Hong, F. and Mangan, J.A. (eds.) *Soccer, women, sexual liberation: kicking off a new era*. London: Frank Cass Publishers, 95–111.

Caudwell, J. (2000) Football in the UK: women, tomboys, butches and lesbians. In: Scraton, S. and Watson, B. (eds.) *Sport, Leisure Identities and Gendered Spaces*. Eastbourne: Leisure Studies Association, 95–110.

Caudwell, J. (2003) Sporting gender: women's footballing bodies as sites/ sights for the (re) articulation of sex, gender, and desire. *Sociology of Sport Journal*, 20(4), 371–386.

Caudwell, J. (2007) Queering the field? The complexities of sexuality within a lesbian-identified football team in England. *Gender, Place and Culture: A Journal of Feminist Geography*, 14(2), 183–196.

Corbett, K. (2009) *Boyhoods: rethinking masculinities*. London: Yale University Press.

Cox, B. and Thompson, S. (2000) Multiple bodies: sportswomen, soccer and sexuality. *International Review for the Sociology of Sport*, 35(1), 5–20.

Cox, B. and Thompson, S. (2001) Facing the bogey: women, football and sexuality. *Football Studies*, 4(2), 7–24. Available from: http://citeseerx.ist.psu.edu/viewdoc/download?doi=10.1.1.536.7157&rep=rep1&type=pdf [Accessed 19 February 2016].

Drummond, M. (2012) Boys' bodies in early childhood. *Australasian Journal of Early Childhood*, 37(4), 107–114.

Dunn, C. and Welford, J. (2015) *Football and the FA Women's Super League: Structure, governance and impact*. London: Palgrave.

Grundlingh, M. (2010) Boobs and balls: exploring issues of gender and identity among women soccer players at Stellenbosch University. *Agenda: Empowering Women for Gender*, 24(85), 45–53.

Hallmann, K. (2012) Women's 2011 football World Cup: the impact of perceived images of women's soccer and the World Cup 2011 on interest in attending matches. *Sport Management Review*, 15(1), 33–42.

Hargreaves, J. (2000) *Heroines of sport: the politics of difference and identity*. Routledge: London.

Harris, J. (2005) The image problem in women's football. *Journal of Sport and Social Issues*, 29(2), 184–197.

Harris, J. (2007) Doing gender on and off the pitch: the world of female football players. *Sociological Research Online*, 12(1). Available from: http://www.socresonline.org.uk/12/1/harris.html [Accessed 5 March 2015].

Hjelm, J. (2011) The bad female football player: women's football in Sweden. *Soccer and Society*, 12(2), 143–158.

Holland, S. and Harpin, J. (2015) Who is the 'girly girl'? Tomboys, hyper-femininity and gender. *Journal of Gender Studies*, 24(3), 293–309.

Howard, J.A. and Hollander, J. (1997) *Gendered situations, gendered selves.* London: Sage.

Jeanes, R. (2005) Girls, football participation and gender identity. In: Bramham, P. and Caudwell, J. (eds.) *Sport, Active Leisure and Youth Cultures.* Eastbourne: LSA, 75–96.

Jeanes, R. (2011) 'I'm into high heels and make up but I still love football': exploring identity and football participation with preadolescent girls. *Soccer and Society*, 12(3) 402–420.

Knijnik, J. and Horton, P. (2013) 'Only beautiful women need apply': human rights and gender in Brazilian football. *Creative Approaches to Research*, 6(1), 60–70.

McCann, A. (2019) World Cup Players Say Muscles and Makeup Mix Just Fine, Thanks. *The New York Times*, 20 June. Available from: https://www.nytimes.com/2019/06/20/style/world-cup-women-hair-gender.html [Accessed 7 October 2019].

Parets, S., Levy M. and Galily, Y. (2011) National and gender identity perceptions among female football players in Israel. *Soccer and Society*, 12(2), 228–248.

Reay, D. (2001) 'Spice Girls', 'Nice Girls', 'Girlies', and 'Tomboys': gender discourses girls' cultures and femininities in the primary classroom. *Gender and Education*, 13(2), 153–166.

Renold, E. (2005) *Girls, boys and junior sexualities: exploring children's gender and sexual relations in the primary school.* London: Routledge Falmer.

Russell, K.M. (2004) On versus off the pitch: the transiency of body satisfaction. *Sex Roles*, 51(9/10), 561–574.

Scraton, S., Fasting, K., Pfister, G. and Brunel, A. (1999) It's still a man's game? The experiences of top-level European women footballers. *International Review for the Sociology of Sport*, 34(2), 99–111.

Scully, D. (1998) Sport and exercise. In: Trew, K. and Kremer, J. (eds.) *Gender and psychology.* London: Arnold, 206–218.

Spade, J.Z. and Valentine, C.G. (2008) *The kaleidoscope of gender: prisms, patterns, and possibilities*, 2nd edition. London: Sage Publications.

Spade, J.Z. and Valentine, C.G. (2017) *The kaleidoscope of gender: prisms, patterns, and possibilities*, 5th edition. London: Sage Publications.

Stirling, L. and Schulz, J. (2011) Women's football: still in the hands of men. *Sport Management International Journal*, 7(2), 53–78.

Tomas, F. (2020) Weight charts, 'fat clubs' and disordered eating: the hidden health crisis in women's football. *The Telegraph*, 23 October. Available from: https://www.telegraph.co.uk/football/2020/10/23/weight-charts-fat-clubs-disordered-eatingthe-hidden-health-crisis/ [Accessed 2 November 2020].

West, C. and Zimmerman, D.H. (1987) Doing gender. *Gender and Society*, 1(2), 125–151.

5 Football families

This chapter is dedicated to the relationships that are formed and consolidated between footballer and parent(s). It is this area of academic research that has yet to receive a great deal of attention in relation to girls' and women's football despite the social significance of family relationships. Broader investigations into sport and family have acknowledged how vital the role of family is in connection with relationships, togetherness and social justice (Trussell et al., 2018). The role that siblings, grandparents, cousins and wider family members play is also significant when examining the experiences of footballing girls and women. Sibling relationships through sport can be a site for bonding but also conflict (Trussell, 2012; Blazo et al., 2014; Taylor et al., 2018). In particular sister and brother relationships in football are often interwoven by complex gender issues (see, Pielichaty, 2021). This chapter will discuss parental and player relationships specifically and will provide a starting point for football family research here.

Women playing football is not a new phenomenon but can be described as having a 'hidden history' (Williams, 2017). The stories of the women's game have been largely ignored in the popular domain but they have lived on through the families of those involved. I am very proud to share that my Great Aunt Patricia Robinson played football for the Yorkshire Copper Works when employed there as a secretary in the 1950s (Photo 5.1).

It was only after my interest in football began did I learn about my Aunt Patricia and her footballing history. Her love for the game is so heart-warming and special to me, it helps me to position the importance of football historically and currently within my own personal timeline. I think it is important at this point to explain a little bit more about my own family background and memories. Huddersfield provides the geographical core at which to start discussions about my family and football history. My parents met in

Photo 5.1 Yorkshire Copper Works Match, Patricia Robinson on the Ball (c1953) courtesy of Helena Pielichaty.

Huddersfield in the 1980s but moved to the East Midlands when I was six months old. Both my parents support Huddersfield Town AFC, a tradition passed down to me, and as I recall happened something like this:

> **Hanya:** I think I support Manchester United (it was the 90s so most people did).
> **Dad:** No you don't, you support Huddersfield Town.
> **Hanya:** Ok.

It is difficult for me to write down the above words. This I promise was my only fandom 'wobble' and I have been a keen Huddersfield Town supporter ever since. Huddersfield Town resided in the lower echelons of the Football League when I first started to follow them and am still amazed that we reached Premier League status in 2017.

Football was never something that was forced upon me when growing up; instead, I discovered the enjoyment through playground football. Once this enjoyment was harnessed it was accommodated very easily into my family network which for the most part loved sport and in particular football (except my brother who had no interest at all in it). This has been examined by Johansen and Green (2019, 427) who discuss the 'sporting trinity' compiled of parents, sports clubs and early-years schooling which provide the foundations for future sporting participation. My parents have both had season tickets at Huddersfield Town in the past and follow the latest updates on Twitter (my mum) or via fan blog sites and newspapers (my dad) to get the most up to date information and news. My mum is an advocate for the girls' and women's game, and as a children's author, she has published a 12-book series entitled *Girls FC*, which was influenced by my own football playing. Both my parents were proud of my playing.

It was my relationship with my dad, though, that was (and still is to a certain extent) affected by football. My father and I carved out a special bond through football, a bond that comes from years and years of football conversations, car trips, emotional coaching, mentoring, support and general love. My father attended every single one of my football games from age 9 until 18 years old when I left for university. He used to wear a red handkerchief as a bandana when he played hockey as a young man which I inherited and wore (either as a headband or around my wrist) when I played football as a lucky motif. My dad didn't mind the horrendous stench of my post-match shin-pads that radiated through the car on the journey home. He would stand pitch-side quietly and assess my games like a qualified and professional coach, only discussing my performance afterwards if I wanted to, awaiting my conversational cues. He was happy to drive us home in silence if I felt I hadn't played well or appease my negative post-game analysis with examples of my creativity or vision instead. Football was 'our thing'.

My dad worked 12 hours a day and in my teenage years, every Thursday evening he would come home from work, quickly change attire and take me straight out to football training and we would return home around 9.30pm. He stayed in the car whilst I trained, eating a sandwich and reading the paper, not to interfere with my performance, waiting for my own post-session analysis on the journey home. I always thought too much about football, I was a very analytical player, stuck in my own head, often to my own detriment. I was supposed to be a striker but I often chose to pass rather than shoot and constantly over-thought goal-scoring situations until I eventually bundled it wide or skied it high. I think it was my own mind that limited my football progression really. My dad knew this about me and would always seek ways to mentor and guide me through my complex cognitive questioning and analysis. This is a trait he still applies in my adult-life, although this time on more boring things like mortgage renewals. It was and is difficult being a football parent; it is so much more than being a glorified taxi driver. The rest of this chapter will focus on the detail and depth of parent-daughter relationships that develop in and around the game of football.

Football families

The significance of football to the player and her family is often interconnected. It is the relationships within and between families that were of significance. Players with salient football identities frequently came from families who also identified strongly with football. The more serious players at the elite level or those with aspirations for professionalism were often from families with strong football identities. Many family members stated they felt lost when the football season finished and did not know how to spend their free time. The importance of football in the lives of these families was tangible and significant. Families of *serious* (salient) footballing daughters were ruled by her football playing in relation to their weekly schedule, financial outgoings and general togetherness. Training and match days tended to occupy two-three days/evenings per week which impacted upon parents' fuel bills for travel, and often families were separated when needing to take children to their individual activities. Parents encouraged their children to be involved in sporting opportunities as the basis for developing long-term economic and social prospects. Many parents valued the role football played in their family lives and viewed it as an all-consuming lifestyle choice, one which was expressed in their everyday routines.

Sport occupied their family identity, which was the case for Barbara who still identified herself as a sportswoman and described her family's love of football as quasi-genetic, 'you're born into it, you haven't got a choice' and 'when you're born into this family you're born into football'. This statement illustrates the ingrained and embedded nature of football in family life; a connection with football was viewed as a certainty and a necessity for being a family member. Family experiences in this study were significantly affected by football participation, families' football identities were salient and football was viewed as having high status (see Burke and

Stets, 2009) in the families' lives. It is understood that 'sporting cultures [are] transmitted through families' (Wheeler, 2011, 235). Daughters born into these families were captivated by football from a young age, and participation was not viewed as a choice but rather as an expectation.

Football was a way of life for these families. Football families worked at maintaining a family football identity; like identities as framed by Burke and Stets (2009), high commitment levels and dedication to providing opportunities and cultivating their daughter's talents consolidated family football identities. Husband Bob and wife Judy had four children, three daughters and one son, all of whom played football. Two of their daughters, including Sabine, played at the highest domestic level in England, and their son gained a football scholarship with a local professional men's team. Daughter Rosie played football recreationally and felt football was part of her family identity. Sabine and father Bob reported family mealtimes as the epicentre for post-match analysis and reflections. The shared 'co-construction of family dinnertime narratives' is an extremely significant ritual to facilitate familial bonding and for expressing both individuality and togetherness as a family (Bohanek et al., 2009, 511). This was certainly the case for this family who used dinnertime as a space to discuss, review and reflect on the activities and experiences of their family through football, which positively impacted upon family functioning (see Buswell et al., 2012). Football provided a focus to family conversations, mediating friendships and fostering a sense of identity and achievement. Football meant so much to the families of this study that it was difficult to express in words, as Bob reports:

> **HP**: What would the Hughes family be like without football?
> **Bob**: Fuh [shocked sound], I don't know...God...dear I don't know.
> **HP**: Can you imagine it?
> **Bob**: No well I can't, I just can't, I just, I dunno, I really don't know, it'd be strange. We'd have a lot of spare time.

When Rosie was asked the same question as her father she replied, 'I think it would be like people without mobile phones'. These sentiments were shared by another family, whereby mother Janet claimed that football 'actually ruled our lives' and transcended each area of their everyday routines including eating regimes and washing kit. This connection between identity and football as expressed through everyday life connects to Stone's (2007) analysis of football fan identities. Stone explains that football is ingrained in the daily routines of those who follow the sport, and this football identity is boundless and crosses into the workplace and family home. These football identities can be all-consuming and Janet admitted she felt 'very free' when her daughters moved to America; this concept of 'free' relates to both the spare time Janet acquired but also the release of pressure from no longer needing to perform so frequently as a 'conspicuous football parent', a concept which will be addressed in the following chapter. It is reported that parents now invest more time in their children's sporting activities and at an earlier age to previous generations (Wheeler and Green, 2014), and therefore, the conclusion of this football commitment can be freeing.

Passionate football families developed and created opportunities for their daughters to participate in football, even at significant financial and personal cost. Hazel and Colin, for example, dedicated their lives to football and made significant efforts to grow the women's game in their locality to assist their daughter's development but also to create opportunities for other players. Parents did know that in the recent past football was recognised as a sport predominantly for boys (see Messner, 2009), and this was something the families in my study were aware of and were proactive in changing. This suggests a different approach to Eliasson's (2011) research that suggested parents were accepting of girls' subordination to boys in sport.

Kay (2000, 151) comments that successful sporting children will come from a 'certain type of family', one which relies on supportive parents and a family willing to dedicate money, time and effort in their child's sporting achievements (see also Post et al., 2018). Football was more than merely an activity or sport; it was an additional member of the family in the sense that it occupied family time and commitment; it had its own place in and outside of the family home. Although football was meaningful to families, the extent of this meaning differed and was dependent on the level of aspiration and achievement of the footballing daughter. Football families cultivated and nurtured their daughter's talent in order for her to progress and develop. Family support (financial/practical/social) offered to daughters did vary from family to family but all of the players involved in my empirical work were able to draw on a level of family support necessary to participate in football. This finding is consistent with previous research examining the financial pressures, time commitment and emotional strains parents experience in attempts to ensure they are providing for and develop their children's sporting needs (Stirrup et al., 2015).

Family members have to accommodate practical, financial and logistical pressures that arise through football participation. Family support is important to the success of girl and women footballers (Stirling and Schulz, 2011) and potentially even more so than for male footballers. Parents of footballing daughters will often have to carve out new opportunities to assist in the development and progression of the sport. Boys' and men's football is ubiquitous in British culture, whereas funding issues, ideological constraints and lack of opportunity can limit girls' and women's chances to engage and progress (see Woodhouse et al., 2019; Pielichaty, 2020). Barriers and challenges to girls' and women's participation in football continue to exist and provide constraints on the development of the game.

It must be noted that some level of family support was provided to players irrespective of their talent or aspirations as a footballer, although higher achieving players experienced greater feelings of pressure. The relationship between pressure and support in these families was complex; the greater support provided to players from parents in terms of opportunities to train and moral guidance increased the chances of players feeling pressure to perform well. Parental pressure is reported as contributing to youth sport dropout in connection with the 'intrapersonal constrains' that young people experience attached to sport (Witt and Dangi, 2018). Arguably, players with salient football selves who had pertinent aspirations to succeed professionally presented challenges for parents; parents in these situations needed to cultivate and nurture their daughter's abilities. Players were provided with logistical, moral and physical support (via spectating) to encourage player's development and well-being. The plethora of support offered by parents of daughters with salient football selves demonstrated the commitment parents had to maintain high-status football identities (see Burke and Stets, 2009).

Career management and logistical challenges negotiated by the parents transcended the standard notion of effective parenting; parents of footballing daughters could be regarded as *performing* 'serious football parenting', as homage to Stebbins' (2008) notion of serious leisure. Serious football parenting demonstrated the way in which parents facilitated their children's sports development in a manner that had significant impact on family lifestyle. The concept of 'serious football parenting' is relatable to the parents in Clarke and Harwood's (2014, 531) study, who referred to their son's football participation as 'a life choice for me'.

Parents and family members watched training sessions and matches and showed support through attendance and spectatorship. Kirsty (U11) the younger sister of Kay (U15) and Zoe (U17) preferred it when both her mum and dad watched her play at weekends but acknowledged that her dad had to balance work along with watching her sisters' play. Miley (U15) explained that both her mum and dad would watch her play but both Miley and Maisy (U17) described the additional pressure they experienced when their parents spectated. It is noted that parental encouragement is essential to young people's prolonged involvement in sport (Haycock and Smith, 2014), and pressure and expectation from parents and siblings may be difficult to negotiate (Willms, 2009; Blazo et al., 2014). Players presented differing relationships with family members; these were often dependent upon perceived levels of support and praise received, as well as how this was delivered.

Another finding was the relationship between players who identified with a salient football self and parental pressure. Players who fully committed to football and viewed it as serious and worthwhile felt greater parental pressure to play well. Pressure levels of recreational players did not feature strongly, whereas elite players absorbed and responded more to this greater sense of pressure. For example, club player Debbie (U15, School) discussed her father watching her play, 'you feel like you've got to play up to their [parents] standards' and some parents were aware of the embarrassment they caused their daughters when watching them play; both Jack and Steve admitted their daughters did not like them watching. This did not, however, stop them continuing to watch and encourage their daughters to develop and progress through football participation.

Family bonding and pride

The distinction between talented, elite-level footballers and school, recreational-level footballers is an important one to make. The players at the academy were of a certain ability level to be accepted into the system, whereas footballers from the school group mostly played for fun on a recreational basis. A recurring theme was how the experiences between those talented and more committed footballers and those who played recreationally transcended into family life. As an exception, some of the players at the academy, although talented and committed to attending, were not sure about their future in football and progressing professionally. It was the players who displayed many of the characteristics that contributed to having salient football selves who had different relationships with their families through football in terms of support and pressure. Due to the level of commitment and additional time and effort needed to foster serious, talented footballers, the sense of pride and family identity relating to football were more pronounced in families of daughters with a salient football self; bonding, however, was a feature in the majority of football families. This raises an interesting question regarding the development of these sporting children: did their family football identity foster a salient footballer or did the salient footballer impact upon family identity? My empirical data provides examples of both pathway developments. Some of the families nurtured and grew their daughter's talent without having an initial passion for the sport, whereas football families already had a pre-existing passion for football to enthuse their children with.

Players found football to be a significant source for bonding with family members, as documented by previous sports-based literature (Wedgwood, 2004; Kay, 2009; Blazo et al., 2014). Bonding was important to the majority of the players, but this was experienced in different ways such as shared family time spent through sports-related travel and fostering relationships based on participation. Pride experienced by parents of professional players or players with professional aspirations was expressed openly. Parents of academy players or older elite players demonstrated pride frequently which was often connected to their daughter's achievements. The achievements of those serious, committed footballers were palpable due to the successes achieved in connection with attendance at high-ranking football events, and therefore, parental pride in these cases was specific and success-related. Examples of these were seen in the U17 academy set-up when Zoe explained that football provided a strong bond between her and her father and he demonstrated great pride in her especially when she attended an England training camp. Parents demonstrated such emotion and pride in connection with their daughter's international status, whether playing for England or representing Great Britain. These successes and the daughter's football identity can be thought to extend into family life, and parental identities can also be developed through this sense of achievement (see Clarke and Harwood, 2014).

This sense of pride also occurred organically at the start of conversations prompted by the initial question of 'how did your daughter get into football?' at which point parents would speak passionately and in minute detail of their daughter's involvement and development in the game. Luke was extremely proud of Lindsey's football playing but explained the busy weekly schedule for the family was tough, it was acknowledged that the dominance of sporting activities of children occupied parental leisure time (Wheeler and Green, 2014). Sport, and in this case football, can and did control the lives of the sports families (see Kay, 2009). Not all players and family members agreed that football was a shared interest which promoted bonding, and bonding and pride were not dependent upon one another; parents still felt a great deal of pride for their daughter's achievements even if they did not directly bond through their daughter's involvement in the game. Parental identities were often directly affected by the success and achievement of their children's sporting identities despite not being sites for bonding for all players. By way of example, Jack explained that his colleagues 'sometimes they have to shut me up' when discussing his daughter's football playing at work. Jack admitted he did not have a strong connection to the sport generally, and therefore, it did not serve as a strong site for bonding with his daughter, but as stated he still felt a great sense of pride due to her playing. The connection between parental identities and children's sporting identities was presented by Michelle's father Colin. Hazel described Colin being 'disappointed' when Michelle retired from football because of the significance to him of the club for which she played; he followed both the men's and women's teams associated with the club name and identified with the team:

> You found it really hard to make that differential really, ok she's only a girl she's playing football but the fact she was playing in the stripes [team colours] meant everything to him.
>
> (Hazel)

Families engaged strongly with football through their daughter's participation which impacted upon parental identity and family identity.

Conclusion

Football is so much more than a game; it is a cultural marker of identity. This chapter discusses the group identity that a family embarks upon through a pre-existing or developed love for football.

Football serves as a vehicle for bonding, whereby parents feel proud of their daughter's sporting achievements. A sense of pressure accompanies these experiences, whether that be parental pressure to cultivate and nurture their daughter's talents, or be pressure on a daughter with a salient football self to perform effectively. Football families are controlled by the sport: with their routines, yearly schedules, daily conversations and identities depending on the existence of football in their lives. The power of sport to those that hold it dear should not be underestimated. The following chapter will build on these discussions and provide a closer examination of parental *visibility* in and around girls' and women's football.

References

Blazo, J.A., Carson, S., Czech, D.R. and Dees, W. (2014) A qualitative investigation of the sibling sport achievement experience. *The Sport Psychologist*, 28(1), 36–47.

Bohanek, J.G., Fivush, R., Zaman, W., Lepore, C.E., Merchant, S. and Duke, M.P. (2009) Narrative interaction in family dinnertime conversations. *Merrill-Palmer Quarterly*, 55(4), 488–515.

Burke, P.J. and Stets, J.E. (2009) *Identity theory*. Oxford: Oxford University Press.

Buswell, L., Zabriskie, R.B., Lundberg, N. and Hawkins, A.J. (2012) The family relationship between father involvement in family leisure and family functioning: the importance of daily family leisure. *Leisure Sciences*, 34(2), 172–190.

Clarke, N.J. and Harwood, C.G. (2014) Parenting experiences in elite youth football: a phenomenological study. *Psychology of Sport and Exercise*, 15(5), 528–537.

Eliasson, I. (2011) Gendered socialization among girls and boys in children's football teams in Sweden. *Soccer and Society*, 12(6), 820–833.

Haycock, D. and Smith, A. (2014) A family affair? Exploring the influence of childhood sport socialisation on young adults' leisure-sport careers in north-west England. *Leisure Studies*, 33(3), 285–304.

Johansen, P.F. and Green, K. (2019) 'It's alpha omega for succeeding and thriving': parents, children and sporting cultivation in Norway. *Sport, Education and Society*, 24(4), 427–440.

Kay, T. (2000) Sporting excellence: a family affair? *European Physical Education Review*, 6(2), 151–160.

Kay, T. (ed.) (2009) *Fathering through sport and leisure*. Oxon: Routledge.

Messner, M.A. and Bozada-Deas, S. (2009) Separating the men from the moms: the making of adult gender segregation in youth sports. *Gender and Society*, 23(1), 49–71.

Pielichaty, H. (2020) Pleasure and the Sanctuary Paradox: Experiences of girls and women playing soccer. *International Review for the Sociology of Sport*, 55(6), 788–806.

Pielichaty, H. (2021) Negotiating sibling relationships in girls' and women's football. In: Trussell, D. and Jeanes, R (eds.) *Families, Sport, Leisure, and Social Justice.* London: Routledge.

Post, E.G., Green, N.E., Schaefer, D.A., Trigsted, S.M., Brooks, M.A., McGuine, T.A., Watson, A.M. and Bell, D.R. (2018) Socioeconomic status of parents with children participating on youth club sport teams. *Physical Therapy in Sport*, 32, 126–132.

Stebbins, R.A. (2008) *Serious leisure.* London: Transaction Publishers.

Stirling, L. and Schulz, J. (2011) Women's football: still in the hands of men. *Sport Management International Journal*, 7(2), 53–78.

Stirrup, J., Duncombe, R. and Sandford, R. (2015) 'Intensive mothering' in the early years: the cultivation and consolidation of (physical) capital. *Sport, Education and Society*, 20(1), 89–106.

Stone, C. (2007) The role of football in everyday life. *Soccer and Society*, 8(2/3), 169–184.

Taylor, R.D., Carson, H.J., & Collins, D. (2018) The impact of siblings during talent development: a longitudinal examination in sport. *Journal of Applied Sport Psychology*, 30(3), 272–287.

Trussell, D.E. (2012) Contradictory aspects of organised youth sport: challenging and fostering sibling relationships and participation experiences. *Youth & Society*, 46(6), 801–818.

Trussell, D.E., Jeanes, R. and Such, E. (eds.) (2018) *Revisiting family leisure research: critical reflections on the future of family centred scholarship.* London: Routledge.

Wedgwood, N. (2004) Kicking like a boy: schoolgirl Australian rules football and bi-gendered female embodiment. *Sociology of Sport Journal*, 21(2), 140–162.

Wheeler, S. (2011) The significance of family culture for sports participation. *International Review for the Sociology of Sport*, 47(2), 235–252.

Wheeler, S. and Green, K. (2014) Parenting in relation to children's sports participation: generational changes and potential implications. *Leisure Studies*, 33(3), 267–284.

Williams, J. (2017) 'The girls of the period playing ball': the hidden history of women's football, 1869–2015. In: Hughson, J., Moore, K., Spaaij, R. and Maguire, J. (eds.) *Routledge handbook of football studies.* Oxon: Routledge, 40–49.

Willms, N. (2009) Fathers and daughters: negotiating gendered relationships in sport. In: Kay, T. (ed.) *Fathering through sport and leisure.* Oxon: Routledge, 124–144.

Witt, P.A. and Dangi, T.B. (2018) Why children/youth drop out of sports. *Journal of Park and Recreation Administration*, 36(3), 191–199.

Woodhouse, D., Fielding-Lloyd, B. and Sequerra, R. (2019) Big brother's little sister: the ideological construction of women's super league. *Sport in Society*, 22(12), 2006–2023.

6 Parenting in girls' and women's football

Parents' involvement in sport has always been complicated and contested, relationships that need to balance positions of care and responsibility alongside those of freedom and empowerment. The media has reported on cases of sporting situations facilitating undesirable parental behaviours (Saner, 2015; O'Riordan, 2019; Richards, 2019; Taylor, 2019), and in one case this resulted in the banning of parents from school sports days (Badshah, 2019). Academically, parenting in sport has been considered in connection with parental competencies and knowledge (Dorsch et al., 2015; Harwood and Knight, 2015), 'good parenting' (Trussell and Shaw, 2012; Pynn et al., 2019), strategy development (Knight et al., 2017) and gender (Dixon et al., 2008; Kay, 2009; Knoester and Randolph, 2019), amongst others. This book, however, is one of the first to offer an in-depth examination of parenting within girls' and women's football. This chapter will provide insight into the everyday lives of parents with footballing daughters. Initially a wider discussion will introduce the topic before presenting findings from my empirical work on the visibility and 'forms' football parents take.

Parenting and sports participation

The way parents facilitate, discuss and celebrate sport in their household and family unit is significant. Sports participation is considered cardinal in displaying a successful version of contemporary family life and child-rearing. Parents' own relationship with sport and physical activity is now also of importance in selecting and demonstrating 'modern family' choices. We know that the extent to which parents themselves participate in sport directly correlates with their children's own participation levels (Rodrigues et al., 2018). Furthermore, cross-generational physical activity facilitates family bonding and opportunities for nurturing, and in general cultivates positive parent-child relationships (Freire et al., 2019). Parents are inclined to invest in their own children's sports participation because of the perceived social and cultural benefits (Wheeler and Green, 2014), in the hope it will build their child's 'sporting capital' (Johansen and Green, 2019, 427). The parent-child relationship in sport demonstrates that young people are 'active co-constructors' of these relationships and not passive to them happening (Strandbu et al., 2019). Family support has also been crucial to the success of women and girl footballers (Stirling and Schulz, 2011; Pielichaty, 2021).

Football parents

Many of the parents were involved with setting up teams to facilitate their daughter's playing or had up-skilled themselves to develop their own credentials as a *football parent* (similar to Knight and Holt's (2013) 'tennis parents'); this was certainly the case for Barbara, Marsha, Bob, John, Colin and Hazel. Through conversations and observations identified in my own work, football parents could analytically and behaviourally be distinguished as *conspicuous* and *inconspicuous* football parents. Clayton and Harris also utilised typologies in their study examining footballers' wives, and 'recognize the dangers of constructing typologies, in that they often imply boundaries where none may exist' (Clayton and Harris, 2004, 332), but nevertheless they found typologies to be valuable to their research. In response to this, the 'extreme' parenting forms developed in my own empirical data were a useful way to explore how parents of football daughters negotiated the football environment. Parents in my work were placed on a Parental Continuum (see Figure 6.1) which afforded them greater mobility than a fixed typology.

Conspicuous and inconspicuous football parents: the Parental Continuum

A conspicuous football parent was one who observably demonstrated a physically visible strong commitment to their daughter's talent and future in the game and displayed (see Finch, 2007) 'serious football parenting'. Within a football context, examples of this were assistance with the organisation of a club, helping to set up match day equipment, volunteering at training and watching training and matches in all circumstances. It was also found that

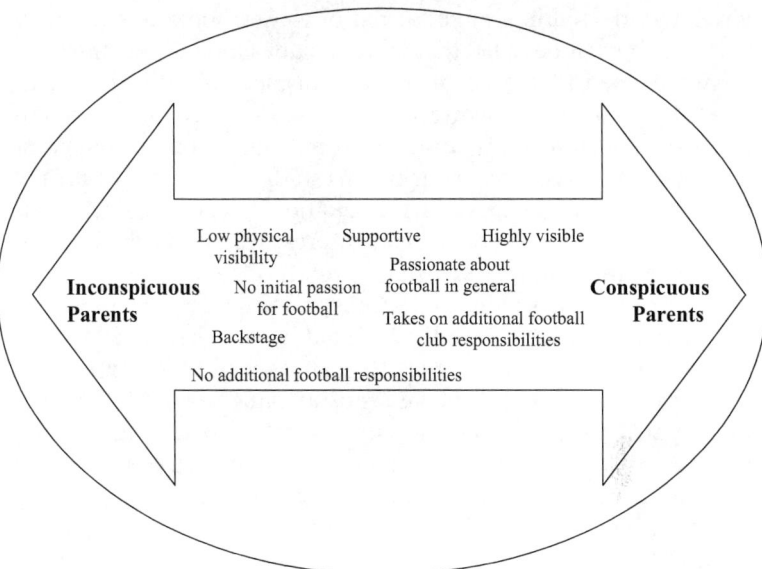

Figure 6.1 The Parental Continuum.

non-public demonstrations of parenting also contributed to the notion of family display, but indirectly. These can be likened to 'backstage' presentations in which parental 'performed' behaviour continues to occur despite the lack of a perceived (more public) audience (see Goffman, 1959). Behind-the-scenes examples included match-day analysis, as observed by parents at the academy, providing additional opportunities for development which parents discussed during conversations and watching professional football with their daughters on television as explained by father, Luke. Thus, Finch's (2007) notion of direct display can be extended to include 'indirect displays' which were also valuable and connected to observable family behaviours. Acts of indirect displays of a conspicuous football parent manifested themselves in public environments, such as during team discussions at training when daughters referenced comments and feedback offered to them previously from their conspicuous football parent(s).

Inconspicuous football parents were those who did not participate in public signs of club support in relation to the wider aspects of club-level football. These parents were not consistently visible at football training and not involved in the organisation and setting-up of matches and training. Often the 'inconspicuous' football parents were at work, waiting in the car out of view or looking after other children. It must be noted that inconspicuous football parents were largely defined by the comments of conspicuous football parents and players. This was significant because the 'absence' of the former symbolised their status as inconspicuous. I did not interview any inconspicuous parents during this study because they were not available on site to engage in conversation. The conspicuous parents were clear about how their own presence and visibility separated them from other, less visible parents.

The words conspicuous and inconspicuous have been used purposefully to indicate a visibility level but by no means does it imply a 'support, love or care barometer'. There may be many reasons why inconspicuous parents were not at pitch-side which cannot be assumed to mean they were unsupportive of their daughter's playing experiences. An inconspicuous parent, therefore, did not necessarily constitute an unsupportive parent but rather one that was not thought of by others to be a conspicuous football parent. Peter joked that some parents on match days seemed to get out of their cars to watch the game just after he and other parents had completed all the jobs, e.g. the nets were put up. Finch's concept of display was highly applicable, and noticed, in particular, by conspicuous football parents who observed and were aware of how their behaviour and engagement were different to those of inconspicuous football parents. Commensurate with Trussell and Shaw's (2012) study, 'good parents' were viewed as those who volunteered and helped with the organisation of the team, whereas absent parents were noticed and criticised by others.

The Parental Continuum marks the extremes of conspicuous and inconspicuous parenting in football, although it is worth noting that many parents would register somewhere in between. Parents classified as closer to the 'conspicuous' or 'inconspicuous' categories may have demonstrated several of the descriptors outlined in Figure 6.1 but not necessarily all of them. My own father would have been classed as an inconspicuous parent on the most-part: staying in his car during training sessions and not having the time to be involved in club committees or take on additional responsibilities. My dad, however, did watch all my competitive fixtures and therefore moved fluidly from inconspicuous parent towards conspicuous parenting for competitive matches. Parents, therefore, can move fluidly along this continuum depending on personal context, time and space. The 'supportive' characteristic occupies a middle-ground as all parents involved in the study demonstrated levels of support for their daughter's participation. Put simply, support was not dependent on being visible. The application of the Parental Continuum allows for movement in and out of parental descriptors and provides space for flexibility and change.

Conspicuous parents: examples from data

Observations and feedback indicated that some parents could be described as 'conspicuous' in relation to their visible determination, commitment, passion for football and extreme public involvement with their daughter's football playing. The conspicuous parents did not necessarily share similar family structures or backgrounds to one another, rather their commonalities lay in their formidable determination to provide for and nurture their daughter's footballing progression. Conspicuous parents were not gender-specific, and data highlights both mothers and fathers who could be identified in this 'form'. Conspicuous football parents invested a great deal of effort in their own relationship and support for their daughter as well as the wider football environment and club.

An important point to make is that conspicuous parents often had daughters with salient football selves and aspirations for professionalism, or indeed had already made it within the higher echelons of the leagues (see Pielichaty, 2019). Some parents also associated with these football identities because football was part of their family lives as well as something simply for their daughters to be immersed in. As stated by Kirsty (U11) 'if we play badly they [parents] shout at us and if we play good they praise us and get us McDonalds'. Football meant a lot to these parents, and their daughter's playing performance reflected their own identities. Josie, a conspicuous mother, was noted for her commitment to football by other parents who would ask her if she was able to take their daughters to training on occasions because they knew that Josie would always attend; she was visible. Josie discussed the need to potentially sell her family home later in Alysha's football career in order to facilitate her daughter's development; as a single parent Josie demonstrated an extraordinary commitment and passion.

Barbara was a conspicuous mum due to the extreme lengths she had taken to provide for her two children. Barbara brought Sarah up as a single parent and worked three jobs in order to provide for her children. Barbara loved football, was an avid supporter and had possessed a season ticket for a men's team from the age of 16 years. Barbara encouraged Sarah to be involved in sport from a young age and believed that sport was the reason why her children did not go 'off the rails'. Sarah explained that her mum was involved in the organisation and running of her team at one point, but as she got older Barbara could not attend many games due to her work commitments (shifting across the Parental Continuum). This indicated that single-parent families do face greater barriers when striving to provide sporting opportunities for their children (see Quarmby and Dagkas, 2010). Conspicuous parents were those who may have a passion for football themselves or a passion for cultivating opportunities for their offspring via sport.

One mother, Janet, is situated close to the conspicuous category on the continuum because of her constant support and commitment to her daughters' football playing but unlike Barbara and Josie her own football knowledge was lacking. Both Suzie and Ellie explained that she 'doesn't really have a clue' because she had never played football but they still listened to her and respected her opinions. Her twin daughters confessed that Janet did not, in general, enjoy football as much as did their dad and three brothers but their mum was a constant source of inspiration to them:

> It's really nice to have her there and I remember my last game for college and she was sitting up there and even though I was having a bit of trouble with it, it was my last home game but I really wasn't feeling it, I was really getting burnt out by this point. Really not enjoying my football but seeing her I thought it's just one last time, just do it, just do it for her. And I played the best I have played all season just because I knew it meant that much to her.
>
> (Suzie)

Janet's dedicated passion, visibility and constant support for her daughters' football participation ensures she is registered closer to the conspicuous parental descriptor. She did not however fulfil the characteristics of 'passionate about football' and taking on additional club duties, and therefore was not positioned at the furthest right position on the continuum.

Craig was very serious about his daughter's football playing, and he would often take Tanya (U15) to the park to play football together and also arranged extra training sessions for Tanya with a coach he knew. Craig felt responsible for Tanya's progression and involvement in football and recalled a girl he knew with abundance of raw talent but without the family support to progress. Craig was very passionate about providing the appropriate environment and experiences for his daughter to flourish in the game, despite that including a £500 monthly petrol bill linked to her playing. Conspicuous parents make up the backbone of grassroots sport; they were frequently visible on the side-line, on a committee panel or volunteering to run a club. These parents were passionate and committed to providing the best opportunities possible for their daughters to enjoy and excel in football.

For some conspicuous parents their identification as a football parent did not shift once their daughter left the sport. Their identities as conspicuous parents continued to extend into the community and professional game as they stayed involved with football. Bob continued to manage and coach women's football teams at the highest level, Hazel and Bob further developed the community's football opportunities for women and girls and Barbara continued to support and follow both the men's and women's game. Unlike a player's football self, which sometimes shifted to a more contingent position when participation stopped, here, conspicuous football parents continued to occupy their dedicated position on the continuum despite their own daughter's ceased involvement.

Inconspicuous parents: examples from data

There were several examples of parents who did not fall into the 'conspicuous' category. These parents can be described as taking a 'backstage' role, a term adopted from Goffman's (1959) dramaturgical conception of identity performance. Backstage depicts those parents who tend to operate behind the scenes in the way they support and facilitate their daughter's football participation. Craig and his wife attended Tanya's games at weekends; however, Tanya's mum spectated to show support for her daughter and not because she particularly liked football. Graeme took Sian to her training sessions but only stood outside and watched if it was not too cold. Peter claimed his wife has no interest in football and 'comes to watch the matches as long as the weather is nice'. Both Steve and Jack did not particularly like football and did not support a professional team, and their only interest in the game came from their daughter's participation. Jack explained he worked most weekends and his wife took Hannah to football games rather than him. Roxanna's dad and brother shouted encouragement from the side-lines when she played but her mum 'likes to stay out of things', although her mother was extremely important to her (School U15):

> She represents more than a mum like, she represents like a strong woman who you can look up to.

Even though Roxanna's mum did not have full involvement in football she remained a highly significant and influential figure in her life. Roxanna's mum represents an inconspicuous, backstage parent, one who is supportive of her daughter's football playing but did not necessarily understand the game or have a genuine interest in the sport. Discussed here by the U15 school players:

Roxanna: My mum only watches it [football] if it's got something to do with David Beckham.
Natalie: Oh yeah.
Debbie: Everybody does, most people watch it when David Beckham's on.

Furthermore, Ellie and Suzie's dad was not fully involved with their football playing but he did provide them with behind-the-scenes support. As a *non-visible* parent, he would prepare supper for them and ran them a bath ahead of their return from football: practical assistance which all helps to inform a player's own football self. Inconspicuous, backstage parents in this study were not devoid of importance or significance in the lives of their daughters but rather were not fully visible within football spaces and/or had no initial passion for the sport.

Sabine's mum, Judy, had an influential role in her football family with regard to football life decisions and the professional game. Judy 'had to' develop into a football fan because her husband and each of her children loved the sport, Sabine explained she was a 'little more confident to give her opinion now' regarding football analysis and technical evaluations. Bob explained that Judy was a very supportive mum and was more football intelligent than she implied because she had watched so much of it and grown into it over the years. The pattern of observations and discussions in relation to inconspicuous parents was that, in general, they did not have an initial passion for the game but had to acquire the basic knowledge of the sport over time. Natalie argued 'my mum is a secret football fan' (School U15) to indicate that inconspicuous parents might not be forward and direct about their understanding of the sport but treasured it as a means of family engagement. Stacey valued her brother's input from the side-lines but considered her mum to be embarrassing, 'she's a mum though isn't she, that's what they do, they just like to get a bit over excited' (School U13).

Conclusion

All players were able to call upon some level of support from their parents, and family life, as previously discussed, was significant to the development of their group and individual identity-building. In this chapter I present to you my interpretation of parental 'forms', namely conspicuous and inconspicuous football parents. Conspicuous parents can be described as dedicated, committed, involved, visible and passionate about football in general. On the contrary, inconspicuous parents are supportive and passionate about their daughter's participation in football but did not necessarily have an initial interest in football and took on a more backstage position. This role was indeed less visible but nonetheless still supportive of their daughter 'doing' football but in a more reserved fashion.

References

Badshah, N. (2019) Primary school bans parents from sports day for bad behaviour. *The Guardian*, 30 June. Available from: https://www.theguardian.com/education/2019/jun/30/primary-school-bans-parents-from-sports-day-for-bad-behaviour [Accessed 11 November 2019].

Clayton, B. and Harris, J. (2004) Footballers' Wives: the Role of the soccer player's partner in the construction of idealized masculinity. *Soccer and Society*, 5(3), 317–35.

Dixon, M.A., Warner, S.M. and Bruening, J.E. (2008) More than just letting them play: parental influence on women's lifetime sport involvement. *Sociology of Sport Journal*, 25(4), 538–559.

Dorsch, T.E., Smith, A.L. and McDonough, M.H. (2015) Early socialization of parents through organized youth sport. *Sport Exercise and Performance Psychology*, 4(1), 3–18.

Finch, J. (2007) Displaying families. *Sociology*, 41(1), 65–81.

Freire, K., Pope, R. and Coyle, J. (2019) What are the drivers of cross-generational physical activity? Exploring the experiences of children and parents. *Journal of Public Health*, 27(5), 591–601.

Goffman, E. (1959) *The presentation of the self in everyday life*. London: Penguin Books.

Harwood, C.G. and Knight, C.J. (2015) Parenting in youth sport: a position paper on parenting expertise. *Psychology of Sport and Exercise*, 16(1), 24–35.

Johansen, P.F. and Green, K. (2019) 'It's alpha omega for succeeding and thriving': parents, children and sporting cultivation in Norway. *Sport, Education and Society*, 24(4), 427–440.

Kay, T. (ed.) (2009) *Fathering through sport and leisure*. Oxon: Routledge.

Knight, C.J., Berrow, S.R. and Harwood, C.G. (2017) Parenting in sport. *Current Opinion in Psychology*, 16, 93–97.

Knight, C.J. and Holt, N.L. (2013) Strategies used and assistance required to facilitate children's involvement in tennis: parents' perspectives. *The Sport Psychologist*, 27(3), 281–291.

Knoester, C. and Randolph, T. (2019) Father-child sports participation and outdoor activities: patterns and implications for health and father-child relationships. *Sociology of Sport Journal*, 36(4), 322–329.

O'Riordan, J. (2019) In children's sport it's the parents who need controlling. *The Irish Times*, 4 July. Available from: https://www.irishtimes.com/sport/in-children-s-sport-it-s-the-parents-who-need-controlling-1.3945635 [Accessed 11 November 2019].

Pielichaty, H. (2019) Identity salience and the football self: a critical ethnographic study of women and girls in football. *Qualitative Research in Sport, Exercise and Health*, 11(4), 527–542.

Pielichaty, H. (2021) Negotiating sibling relationships in girls' and women's football. In: Trussell, D. and Jeanes, R. (eds.) *Families, sport, leisure, and social justice*. London: Routledge.

Pynn, S.R., Dunn, J.G.H. and Holt, N.L. (2019) A qualitative study of exemplary parenting in competitive female youth team sport. *Sport, Exercise and Performance Psychology*, 8(2), 163–178.

Quarmby, T. and Dagkas, S. (2010) Children's engagement in leisure time physical activity: exploring family structures as a determinant. *Leisure Studies*, 29(1), 53–66.

Richards, V. (2019) Gary Lineker wants parents to stop shouting at their kids from football pitch sidelines. *Huffington Post*, 26 September. Available from: https://www.huffingtonpost.co.uk/entry/gary-lineker-wants-parents-to-stop-shouting-at-their-kids-from-the-sidelines_uk_5d8c7e19e4b0019647a36407?guccounter=1&guce_referrer=aHR0cH M6Ly93d3cuZ29vZ2xlLmNvVnLw&guce_referrer_sig=AQAAACx LEz-h_jetDgehImUxW3E51shAnX8mBMOIkr8HdVlCnUeWCypE f2zWTNNBWlzJxAts31ZkDqzOx1QGwWCRfjcs6nM6zyhNJn6jB 0cMA5WN-C8wRKzeDs2L-QT3BD-eS4-_pFx13NSWK0UDcB c34rZ88cCTIPAj3_Lx7E2vd6y3[Accessed 11 November 2019].

Rodrigues, D., Padez, C. and Machado-Rodrigues, A.M. (2018) Active parents, active children: the importance of parental organized physical activity in children's extracurricular sport participation. *Journal of Child Health Care*, 22(1), 159–171.

Saner, E. (2015) Are pushy parents putting children off sport? *The Guardian*, 12 September. Available from: https://www.theguardian.com/sport/2015/sep/12/are-pushy-parents-putting-children-off-sport [Accessed 27 December 2020].

Stirling, L. and Schulz, J. (2011) Women's football: still in the hands of men. *Sport Management International Journal*, 7(2), 53–78.

Strandbu, A., Stefansen, K., Smette, I. and Sandvik, M.R. (2019) Young people's experiences of parental involvement in youth sport. *Sport, Education and Society*, 24(1), 66–77.

Taylor, A. (2019) Strict rules and social pressure stamp out bad behaviour among spectators. *The Sydney Morning Herald*, 4 August. Available from: https://www.smh.com.au/national/nsw/strict-rules-and-social-pressure-stamp-out-bad-behaviour-among-spectators-20190802-p52d9i.html [Accessed 11 November 2019].

Trussell, D.E. and Shaw, S.M. (2012) Organized youth sport and parenting in public and private spaces. *Leisure Sciences*, 34(5), 377–394.

Wheeler, S. and Green, K. (2014) Parenting in relation to children's sports participation: generational changes and potential implications. *Leisure Studies*, 33(3), 267–284.

7   Gendered parenting

This chapter examines gendered approaches to parenting through sport. Historically, it was fathers and their sons who bonded over football participation as a joint venture to instigate and consolidate masculine identity-building (see Jeanes and Magee, 2011). This book provides an interesting twist on this normative position because it is fathers and daughters experiences of football participation that are of importance here. Does this mean that masculine identities are not consolidated through female football participation? How does the father-daughter relationship function through girls' and women's football participation?

Traditionally, fathers were believed to have a greater impact on their children's sports participation (Greendorfer and Lewko, 1978). A study by Raudsepp and Viira (2000) found that male adolescents' activity levels were most affected by fathers' and brothers' activity levels as opposed to female adolescents' activity levels, which were related to both parents' and siblings' own activity levels. This demonstrates the effect that gender, rather than position in the family hierarchy, has upon sports participation. Sport can serve as an emotional bond between daughter and especially father, which occurs through playing, watching and/or talking about sport (Wedgwood, 2004; Harrington, 2009). Leisure has been an important medium for fathers to develop and nurture their relationships with their children, and has a special significance for them (Kay, 2009). Blazo et al. explain that 'many of the participants spoke of the specific role of their fathers in relation to sports participation' (Blazo et al., 2014, 42).

It is recognised that 'daughters who play sport occupy a complex and potentially ambiguous position in relation to sport and in relation to their fathers' (Willms, 2009, 126). Willms' research is very engaging and reports on the complex and dynamic relationship between fathers and daughters within a sport setting. Willms argues that daughter-father relationships (more so than son-father relationships) in sport require greater effort, and that the daughter may be vulnerable when seeking paternal approval. For example, fathers and daughters bond through sport and create a unique relationship, whereby fathers take on the multiple roles of fan, trainer and coach and commit a lot of time and effort to the attachment. The daughters, however, feel their father's love is dependent on their success and want to achieve to impress. Thus, daughters experience conflicting emotions as a result of this special bond: enjoying the attention it brings but also feeling pressurised to succeed to please their fathers.

Kay warns of the overly competitive and abusive characteristics some fathers can display but maintains that involved fathers have the opportunity and capacity to 'resist and transform existing gender hierarchies in and surrounding sport' (Kay, 2009, 121). By fathers being more involved and available within their children's leisure experiences, Kay explains that fathers can challenge the stereotypical view of non-caring and disengaged fathers through shared leisure. Valentine (1997) acknowledges that a child has different relationships with each parent. Fathers are more concerned about their children conforming to normative gender-appropriate behaviour (McHale et al., 2003) and are more inclined to differentiate between boys and girls (Lytton and Romney, 1991). Corbett (2009) states boys identify more with their fathers; furthermore, heterosexual fathers play a key role in developing their sons' masculinity, which reinforces the father's own masculine identity (Kane, 2008).

The dominant cultural understanding of mother is still one of caregivers, and Valentine (1997) illustrates that mothers are viewed by their children as responsive and sympathetic whilst fathers are viewed as powerful and autocratic. Valentine also refers to a 'mismatch' between this cultural valuation of mother as perfect caregiver and that of a contemporary career woman. Mothers, in Valentine's study, explained they were very aware of societal pressures to act and behave in a certain way to ensure motherhood was performed *correctly*.

Examinations of parenting roles through sports show that mothers take on 'behind-the-scenes' roles connected to family organisation, transportation and project management, whereas fathers take on authoritarian, dominant roles in and around sport such as coach, official and board member (Dixon et al., 2008; Claringbould and Adriaanse, 2015). The position of 'intensive mothering' (Hayes,

1996) can be applied to 'soccer moms' (Swanson, 2009), whereby mothers are proactive in carving out the most beneficial path for a child's success no matter the personal, financial and logistical sacrifice to the parent. How these research patterns relate to parents of footballing daughters (rather than sons) will be explored in the following section.

Gendered parenting in girls' and women's football

My examination into the lives of girls and women footballers and their families did not initially focus on the gendered displays of football parents but this did appear in my fieldwork. I thought it would be useful to cite these findings here to facilitate discussion surrounding how women and men negotiate their daughter's footballing experiences. The data I collected on this topic specifically was not vast enough to generalise, and therefore, this chapter is presented as an introductory 'taster' to this subject area. These data are not here to typecast 'all' mothers or 'all' fathers but instead to add to sociological debate considering potential gendered behaviours of mothers and fathers in and around girls' and women's football in England.

Fathers were more visible at the academy site and those I spoke to carved out very significant and special bonds with their daughters through football playing. Many fathers in the research demonstrated a variety of mixed characteristics from both the conspicuous and inconspicuous descriptors, whereas the majority of mothers discussed in this study were more polarised in character. Non-visible mothers, as described by their daughters or partners, displayed characteristics of inconspicuous parents much more strongly than fathers in this research as demonstrated by the following set of quotes:

> She only supports Arsenal really, because she's from Arsenal.
>
> (Sian, U11)

> Mums tend to drop them off and go.
>
> (Grandma Elma)

> She [mum] likes to stay out of things.
>
> (Roxanna, School U15)

It is worth remembering that inconspicuous parents are largely described indirectly by others because of their lack of visibility, and therefore, claims made are general and do carry with them a level of assumption.

Traditionally, fathers not mothers have expertise in sports and therefore, it is fathers who often developed their children's sporting talents by mediating role of coach, manager and mentor (Coakley, 2006). This was the case for many of the fathers here, who laid claim to the nurturing and developmental roles of their daughters in football. It must be noted that all of the mothers involved in the family interviews were categorised as conspicuous football parents, but this was not mirrored by the academy observations or school site discussions. The families who were part of the study were known for being 'football families', and the mothers interviewed in the majority of families were cardinal to the family football identification. Distinct to this, not as many mothers were visible at the academy training sessions for direct interviews and player responses at both the academy and school sites did not focus heavily on their mother's involvement.

Both fathers and mothers who were identified as conspicuous football parents shared similar characteristics of being visibly committed, involved and engaged with their daughter's participation. Conspicuous football mothers and some conspicuous fathers were concerned with the ability and progression of their own daughter as well as advancing sporting opportunities available to others, including the growth of girls' and women's football more broadly. This manifested in developing and running community clubs and school opportunities and achieving coaching qualifications to advance girls' and women's football. The mothers involved in this differed to the behind-the-scenes, seemingly ignorant mothers described by Claringbould and Adriaanse (2015), whereas conspicuous football mums in my empirical data were positioned as coaches, club developers, board members and activists. Furthermore, the conspicuous mums also provided contrasting findings to the 'team moms' in Messner and Bozada-Deas' (2009) research who were often assigned 'housekeeping' tasks and were overlooked for coaching roles. The mothers from my empirical data may have found it easier to enter these roles because it was in girls' and not boys' football and because of this negotiated a different type of 'borderwalk' (Thorne, 1993). Women, in this instance mothers, were not 'trespassing' into *men's* or *boys'* territory but actually entering the masculine arena of football via an alternative route.

Conspicuous football fathers demonstrated concern with their own daughter's progression and well-being and viewed their daughter's personal development as paramount. This challenges previous research which suggests 'fathers perceived that sport had more value for their sons' (Fredricks and Eccles, 2005, 13). These conspicuous football fathers often used to play football themselves, already had a passion for the sport and in most cases introduced their daughters to football initially (similar to Stirling and Schulz, 2011).

Fathering through girls' and women's football

Commensurate with research by Dixon et al. (2008) fathers dominated the coaching side of their daughter's football experience, but in my fieldwork, this manifested as both 'real' coaches and self-labelled coaches. The technical and strategic side of the game was also important for fathers as consistent with Claringbould and Adriaanse's (2015) previous research. Daughters and dads would share tactical information to assist in matches and training. The dads involved in this research certainly found fatherhood complex, in the sense that they needed to balance their daughter's football playing with work and home life commitments and also take on the roles of coach, mentor, psychologist and friend all under the umbrella of dad. But it was not contradictory as suggested by Kay (2009); often the dads found fatherhood and their daughter's participation easy to accommodate and provided care and emotional supporting roles through the medium of football. These fathers were able to negotiate and combine their role of orthodox and inclusive masculinities in a contemporary and liberal way (Adams, 2011; Gottzén and Kremer-Sadlik, 2012).

Peter's daughter, Olive (U13), was a very self-critical and analytical player, and Peter described having to mentor and coach her to view the game more holistically rather than concentrating on her own individual errors. Peter would be creative in his parenting in order to build up her confidence and self-esteem; after one match on the drive home, Olive wanted some money to buy something from the service station. Peter explained she was allowed 50 pence for every positive comment she could make about her performance, Olive earned £1.50 and this process seemed to lift her mood. Peter was taking on the role of sports psychologist and coach in terms of cognitive training and positive thinking to balance an assessment of athletic performance with caring fatherhood (Gottzén and Kremer-Sadlik, 2012). Fathers drew upon their own biographical experiences to inform and guide their own daughter's participation in the game. Wanting to preserve their daughter's love of the game was a priority for fathers and was often seen as a fine balance between nurturing talent and ring-fencing enjoyment and passion for the sport. Marsha, Hope's (U11) mum, explained that she enrolled on a football level 1 coaching course to engage with football at the school she worked at. Marsha claimed she wanted to do more and believed as a mother involved in particularly school football you needed to show above and beyond the interest rates of dads to be taken seriously. Marsha was involved with some of the U9 coaching sessions during the season as part of her professional development for her coaching badge.

Unlike Marsha and some of the other dads who were qualified coaches, many fathers became honorary coaches throughout the time of their daughter's participation. Honorary coaches can be understood as those fathers who do not have any official coaching qualifications but still feel they have the required experience and expertise to advise, mentor and guide their daughter's football playing. Debbie (U15) explained her dad requests, 'listen to me and not the coach but I just ignore him'. John, a 'real' coach, admitted he found it hard not to coach his children when he watched them play, he explained 'dad goes out of the window and turns into coach'. Bob discussed the difficulty of balancing fatherhood with being a 'real' football coach and said he would never let his daughters win a football award from him as he did not want to be perceived as biased. Fathers were very valuable to the players, and their opinions and advice were often regurgitated and reflected upon during football experiences by their daughters. One U11 player claimed, 'I know what the offside is, my dad taught me' and when the U11 group was asked to provide feedback on the previous match, a player opened with the line 'my dad says...' demonstrating the important educational and mentoring role fathers played in their daughter's lives. Fathers' opinions had gravitas, for example Kelly (U13) informed her teammates 'my dad says it's the best game we've played' as if he held an authoritative position in making the judgement. Debbie (U15) explained that sometimes her dad turned into a coach and criticised her, and it could make her feel 'a bit rubbish'. The coaching role dads took on was crucial to their relationships surrounding football as it allowed for a frequent football dialogue between father and daughter. Tiffany (U13) explained that her dad was the only one in her family interested in football and encouraged her to play. Tiffany and her dad had important pre-match discussions, 'he says like be strong and don't let them like push you around' which was a way of coaching and mentoring Tiffany.

The importance of the father-daughter relationship was one theme which shone through. The multiple and frequent references made by players about fathers rather than mothers highlighted the importance of this relationship throughout. Sian (U11) clearly demonstrated the importance of her father's involvement in her football playing:

HP: Do your mum and dad like football as well?
Sian: Dad does.
HP: Does your mum not like it?
Sian: Um, she only supports Arsenal really, because she's from Arsenal.
HP: Who do you talk to most in your family about football?
Sian: Mainly my dad.
HP: Do you, how come?
Sian: Coz he gives me tips and he used to play for a team.
HP: Did he?
Sian: When he was younger.
HP: Do you like it when your dad gives you tips?
Sian: Yeah, it helps me with my football and when he helps me it helps me like in my matches. And like my dad made me do *scanning* and I got 5 because I *scanned* on Saturday and saw Mercedes up front so I curled it up front and then passed it to Paris and Paris just smashed it into the goal and that was one nil.
HP: And that was working with your dad to do that tactic?
Sian: Yeah he's been teaching me how to curl a ball now.

Due to her father's previous football experience he was deemed more qualified to offer tactical guidance, rather than her mum (see also Coakley, 2006), who only supported Arsenal because she was from the area, to offer strategic advice. Sian, who demonstrated a salient football self, enjoyed the sense of achievement when applying her learning to match situations. In this example Sian's dad could be viewed as an extension of the coaching team at the academy and assisted Sian in her development outside of football training.

The 'expert' coaching and technical advice, attributed to fathers, was recycled in the public domain at football training which increased the *narrative visibility* of fathering in football and the importance of their support and relationships. By fathers also being more physically present at training and in football spaces, the significance of their support is consolidated by their physical visibility.

Overall, relationships with fathers were significant and affectionate, often based on performance development, strategy and confidence boosting.

Pre-and post-match analyses were considered very significant parts of the football cycle in which conspicuous dads could put into use their amateur coaching role and self-made managerial prowess. It is these areas of fatherhood which connect to orthodox masculinities and the need for fathers to develop and improve their daughter's performance (see Gottzén and Kremer-Sadlik, 2012). This connection is made in the sense that fathers could take on a dominant 'teacher' or 'coach' role and instruct and guide their daughters in attempts to boost performance and achievement. These dominant roles traditionally associated with men and masculinity (Messner and Bozada-Deas, 2009) continue to connect with orthodox masculinities.

The greater visibility of fathers in comparison with mothers within the football environment nevertheless crystallised the continued dominance of men in and around football. Sport and leisure are viewed as valuable spaces for fathers to create and solidify relationships with their children (Kay, 2009; Jeanes and Magee, 2011) in a manner which does not compromise their masculine image (Such, 2009). Fathers, in this study, were able to display a nurturing and caring side towards their children within the football environment at the same time as consolidating their masculine pride through this connection to sport. This is consistent with Jeanes and Magee's (2011) study examining football sons and fathering, wherein the sons' achievements and performance directly impacted upon fathers' sense of identity. Fathers' masculine identities were also consolidated here through their daughter's participation and achievements. Fathers were 'doing' gender (as theorised by West and Zimmerman, 1987) and expressed their masculinity by being involved in the game and 'doing football'. This was demonstrated by taking their daughters to training, watching from the side-lines, offering advice, encouraging progression and sharing in their daughter's sporting achievements. Fathers are more likely to take an interest and volunteer in masculine sports (Trussell and Shaw, 2012), which could explain the dominant visibility of fathers within this study.

Football fathers were closely linked to the 'useful dad' and 'fully involved dad' categories of Hatter and others' (2002) research. This was demonstrated through their high commitment levels towards their daughter's sporting pursuit as well as working with their partners logistically to manage their busy family schedules. These high commitment levels also demonstrated salient identities (Stryker, 1980; Burke and Stets, 2009), whereby fathers prioritised their daughter's football participation and their own role within the family football environment. Leisure has been described as a site for father-child bonding which can simultaneously demonstrate contemporary caring fatherhood whilst upholding fatherly masculinity (Such, 2009). When fathers co-create shared leisure experience with their sons they are able to create and reinforce each other's masculine identities; however, this was not the case for fathers of football-playing daughters. Daughters did not need to reinforce a shared masculinity with their father through joint leisure experiences; however, the significant father-daughter relationship through football meant men continued to dominate entry to the sport and the associated surveillance within it. This domination refers to the high visibility and importance of dads within the football spaces and in terms of encouraging initial entry into the sport. Regarding surveillance, fathers guided and monitored their daughter's progression through football in relation to post-match analysis and 'coaching' advice. As demonstrated by the following observations and quotes:

Dads standing around the perimeter of the training space.
Dad in the goal for the U11 girls shooting against him before official start of practice.
I think girl's football is less important for the girls that play than the dads that want them to be playing.

(Hazel)

Approximately 70% of the parents at match days are dads.

(Peter)

Clare's dad tells her to quieten down in the warm up.
No he [brother] just listens in to what me and my dad say.

(Esme, U15)

Fathers controlled the football spaces. Dads, however, facilitated their masculinity in a modified and inclusive way to accommodate their daughter's participation. Masculine identity was maintained through the engagement with the traditionally masculine sport of football. Fathers dominated numbers at the academy and this connectivity to sport contributed to masculinity maintenance, in accord with research on boys' soccer (Claringbould and Adriaanse, 2015).

Men continue to be the gatekeepers and managers of girls' and women's football (as consistent with UEFA, 2015, 2017; FIFA, 2019) albeit in supportive ways which facilitated family identity and parental bonding. Men and boys, whether family members or coaches/teachers were significant influencers on the players' initial take up of football (Table 7.1).

As the below table illustrates, from the players who explicitly stated how they became involved in football, the majority reported it was due to male encouragement. Fathers, brothers and male friends continued to be the main inspiration for girls taking up football in line with previous accounts (Lopez, 1997; Scraton et al., 1999; Stirling and Schulz, 2011).

Fathers, however, negotiated a dual role of orthodox and inclusive masculinity (see Gottzén and Kremer-Sadlik, 2012). Orthodox masculinity describes the competitive desire for fathers to see progress and improvement from their sporting children, whereas 'inclusive masculinity' (Anderson, 2009) involves development and care. These two masculinities co-existed in my findings, and fathers had to balance their ambition to see their daughters advance and

Table 7.1 Influential Figures for Football Participation Take Up

Influencer	Relationship	Number	Total
Male	Dad	10	23
	Brother	5	
	Dad and brother	2	
	Granddad and dad	1	
	Neighbour	1	
	Teacher	1	
	Cousin	1	
	Boys recreationally (school/park)	2	
Female	Mum	1	8
	Teacher	1	
	Friend	2	
	Grandma	1	
	Sister	1	
	Coach	2	
Unspecified or both male and female influence	Parents	1	3
	Coach	1	
	Brother and female friend	1	
		Total	34

achieve as well as being nurturing and encouraging. Alice's dad did not have any sons and therefore encouraged Alice to play football in order to bond and feel closer to her:

> When I was little, because it was just me and my sister my dad's always wanted someone, you know like, a guy thing. So like dads normally have like little boys, and they bond and everything. But so I was like proper into football and he used to play and then he kinda of got me into it.
>
> (School U13)

In this case football was viewed as a shared activity that fathers found valuable to facilitate bonding and foster a shared love of sport. Alice could be viewed as a *surrogate son*; her leisure experience was adapted to replace a potential gap in her father's life. Or rather, Alice's dad, like so many others, demonstrated and upheld a contemporary version of masculinity typified by being more liberal, inclusive and emotionally engaged (Adams, 2011). Stirling and Schulz (2011) argue that a joint love of football cements the daughter-father bond. Jenny explained that as well as her own father, the fathers of football-playing boys in her village were influential and encouraging figures in her own development when she was younger. Involved fathers have the ability to fight and in turn transform traditional gender hierarchies linked to sport (Kay, 2009), and this was evidenced in the current study in part by the support and development opportunities fathers provided to their daughters to help them excel in football. Simultaneously however the fathers continued to crystallise their dominant position within women's football by operating as gatekeepers to the game and being visible.

Fathers did not demonstrate or indeed discuss the kinds of acts of aggression or abuse which featured strongly in Jeanes and Magee's (2011) research. A parent in passing did recall some pitchside negativity but this was reported as an isolated case. Fathers explained the additional training opportunities they provided to their daughters in order to encourage further development. In general, the family conversations and discussions about football participation and future success were devoid of aggression and abuse. Fathers in this study did not express overt signs of masculinity, traditionally identified through displays of machismo, chauvinism and misogyny (Hughson, 2000). Instead, fathers showcased more contemporary styles of masculinity such as being liberal, inclusive and physically and emotionally engaged (Adams, 2011). Contemporary masculinity was demonstrated by bonding with their daughters through football, providing additional support, expressing pride, nurturing their daughter's talent and enjoying the experience with them.

As opposed to the talent development set-up within the boys' and men's game, the dream of professional football and a career in football did not have the same impact for all the girls here. Older players discussed combining football playing 'on the side' of their future career, and one player in the study who did earn a wage from football explained it was not widely available at all levels of the game. Some parents of elite-level younger players were sceptical about their daughter's future in the game and acknowledged it was difficult to focus on football as a genuine career path. This was of significant difference to the research on fathering in boys' football in connection with career prospects (Jeanes and Magee, 2011).

Many dads were extremely significant to their daughter's footballing experiences and often instrumental in their progression and enjoyment of the sport. The visibility of fathers may be possible due to the behind-the-scenes support from mothers. For example, Graeme explained his wife would come to all of Sian's games if they could better balance their time between their two children. Fathers provided guidance, knowledge and moral support for their daughters, for example, Poppy started playing football to make her dad proud (School U13). Most of players in this study described sharing a strong bond with their fathers based on their football participation and a shared love for the game, which is congruous with previous studies (Wedgwood 2004; Willms, 2009; Stirling and Schulz, 2011). This strong bond could be explained by the dedication and time fathers spent with their footballing daughters. This shared bond started early in some cases, as Sabine recalled, 'I used to love it; it used to be the highlight of my week was to go and watch my dad play football on a Saturday'.

The strength of the relationship between father and daughter was powerful and enduring. Older players in this study who continued to play the sport discussed the strength of their relationships with their fathers which were sustained and consolidated through a continued football presence. Bob, for example, played football himself until he was 38 years old and then became involved in coaching girl's football because of his three daughters. Michael admitted that his three daughters were all *daddy's girls*, and he understood that it was his influence and support that encouraged them to play. Similar to the work on fathering through sport (Kay, 2009) and fathering through football (Jeanes and Magee, 2011), football here provided a site for fathers to formulate, develop and nurture relationships with their child or children. This chapter acknowledges the 'specific role' (Blazo et al., 2014, 42) and unique relationship (Willms, 2009) fathers and daughters share within sport.

Michael explained the deep guilt he felt when he did not manage to watch each of his daughters in their matches at the weekend because they all played at the same time. His tactic was to stand at a corner post, equidistant to each pitch in an attempt to watch three games at once. Kay (U15) his middle daughter was notably upset if he watched more of Zoe's (U17) games and balancing his attention was a complex challenge for Michael: this issue has been highlighted in previous research (Harwood and Knight, 2009; Blazo et al., 2014) which focused on parental bias, and the stress linked to distributing equal attention between children. This also aligned to Willms' (2009) research which analysed the multiple roles fathers took on when facilitating their daughters' sports participation as well as the experience of conflicting emotions. In particular, Willms noted that at times daughters might feel that fatherly love was dependent on their sporting achievement and they felt pressure to succeed because of this. Fathers in my empirical research did experience complex emotions of guilt and pride when watching their daughters play. Through discussions with players they also felt pressure to perform well and make their parents proud. It is these instances which demonstrated the dual fathering role of inclusive and orthodox masculinities (Gottzén and Kremer-Sadlik, 2012). Despite this, there was no indication in this study that players felt that fatherly love was dependent on the daughter's success in football, but rather it was associated with a sense of pride and general satisfaction.

Mothering through girls' and women's football

Mothering in association with girl's and women's football has not, to my knowledge, been previously examined and therefore presents a very interesting aspect of this book. Much of the information in connection with mum's roles through football does start with comparison points to fathers. It was a shared passion for football which differentiated many of the fathers from the (inconspicuous) mothers, as Esme (U15) explained:

HP: Do they ever come and watch you play football?
Esme: My brother does.
HP: Do you like him watching you play?

Esme: Yeh, he doesn't really do much. Just stands there and watches.

HP: Do you have a conversation after about the game at all?

Esme: What with my brother?

HP: Yeah.

Esme: No he just listens in to what me and my dad say.

HP: So is it mostly you and your dad who kinda analyse it all and do all that stuff?

Esme: My mum like doesn't really understand football, well she does but because my dad like is really passionate about sport.

All of Esme's family supported her football playing and would watch her play as a unit but this football engagement was dominated by Esme and her father. This is consistent with Haycock and Smith's (2014) findings which cite motherly involvement as important in terms of organisation and facilitating experiences of sport but not necessarily through direct involvement. The traditional responsibilities of women in the family environment have been found to be highly resistant to change (Hughes, 2002). These mothers were not characterised by their daughters or other football parents as visible football parents and therefore were more likely to consolidate the view of mothers as behind-the-scenes operators. As referenced previously, the conspicuous football mums were however more directly involved in attempts to foster new ways of thinking about football mothers.

It is noted that sport fosters an emotional bond between father and daughters in relation to playing, watching and speaking about sport (Wedgwood, 2004). Due to this emotional connection it has been argued that daughter's relationships with their mothers suffer (Stirling and Schulz, 2011; Claringbould and Adriaanse, 2015), which was not found in my empirical data. Graeme explained that Sian is a *daddy's girl* in relation to football but for everything else she goes to her mum. This example consolidates the general findings from my fieldwork that very much highlighted the strength in relationship between father and daughter but not at the detriment of mother and daughter relationships. In some cases, players bonded more closely with their mums through football, and in other cases, their mothers took on more supportive roles to facilitate their daughter's football playing. The families often operated as a unit, a team in which each family member worked together to ensure their daughter was supported and nurtured.

It is thought mothers play a key role in the sport socialisation of their children but in differing ways to fathers (Haycock and Smith, 2014). The concept of a good mother is often linked to 'sacrifice and availability to all family members at all times' (Spowart, Hughson and Shaw, 2008, 188), and this involves domesticity, care and nurturing. Stirrup, Duncombe and Sandford (2015) refer to the phrase 'intensive mothering' as being applicable to both mothers and fathers who provide a plethora of developmental opportunities for their children in relation to physical activity. Conspicuous mothers and fathers provided additional and informal opportunities for their daughters to develop and excel. Mums, in particular, provided opportunities for wider community development as well as fostering their own daughter's talent. This finding, however, was taken from a small sample of mothers and further investigation into this is needed. Being a conspicuous football mother was not about being the sports chauffeuse (Dixon et al., 2008), managing the club canteen or being footballing ignorant (Claringbould and Adriaanse, 2015).

Mothers were observed discussing tactics and performance between one another during training sessions and those who were visible typically possessed a passion for the sport. For some mums this enjoyment of the game occurred as a result of their daughter's participation and was not necessarily present beforehand. She's 'into it now' said Kay (U15) when discussing her mum's increased interest in the game. In some cases, however, it was mothers who provided the developmental support for daughters to play. Gretchen's (U13) mum, a former player herself, encouraged her to go to the academy after Gretchen started playing football at school. Sport has the capacity to resist as well as recycle traditional gender stereotypes linked to motherhood and fatherhood (Trussell and Shaw, 2012). In my study conspicuous mums directly attacked the concept of supportive but behind-the-scenes mothering which defies the generalisation that fathers are automatically the expert parents in relation to sports (Coakley, 2006; Claringbould and Adriaanse, 2015). In contrast to American 'soccer-moms' (Swanson, 2009), mothers here resisted normative forms of traditional motherhood by entering the masculine domain of football via their daughter's participation in the sport. The mothers in Swanson's (2009) study were trapped by the rigid concept of motherhood and were 'constantly on call for their job as soccer mom' (Swanson, 2009, 351), whereas mums in the current examination did not seem to view their role in their daughter's participation as a 'job' or a duty but rather as enjoyable and culturally significant.

Janet discussed the importance of her presence at football training for her daughters, who initially were shy but became more confident with her there; she was often the only mother on the sideline. Janet admitted that football 'brought a lot to me' and found football to be a very social place and a space for bonding with her daughters. Mothering through football appeared to be a mutually beneficial relationship in which both mother and daughter gained and advanced their togetherness through participation. Gearson (2010) claimed that children take on an active role in their own development and it is argued that this is also the case for parents, not just children. Parents were active in shaping and creating their own roles in relation to their children and the shared experiences they enjoyed. Naomi (Michelle's sister) described her parents as 'mum was the boss; dad was just laid back'; however, both were equally important to Michelle's football progress but in differing ways. As consistent with the other conspicuous football parents, Michelle's mother progressed and supported the growth of the women's game whilst Michelle's father assisted her with this aim and offered his football fandom and experience of the game. Conspicuous parents were also instrumental in providing avenues for social change and 'gender justice' through their commitment to girls' football experiences in the form of everyday activism.

Conclusion

This chapter has drawn together some insights into the gendered nature of parenting in and around girls' and women's football. This is a particularly complex area of analysis due to the deeply ingrained gendered matrix of both family and football. Here fathers and mothers played significant roles in the development and progression of their daughter's footballing journeys, albeit in differing ways. The physical and narrative visibility of fathers in and around football continues to consolidate the male-dominance of the sport. Conspicuous mums, however, actively challenge the previous notions of behind-the-scenes and ignorant mothering. It is highly important that further research is conducted into the gendered displays of parenting in sporting spaces, because this chapter is rather limited by the way in which the research was conducted. I have relied on discussions predominantly with players and conspicuous football parents to shape my valuations of gendered parenting and of course more needs to be done. That aside, this chapter has presented a glimpse into a relatively new and original research area and has outlined the seemingly gendered, parental approaches to girls' and women's football.

References

Adams, A. (2011) 'Josh wears pink cleats': inclusive masculinity in the soccer field. *Journal of Homosexuality*, 58(5), 579–596.

Anderson, E. (2009) *Inclusive masculinity: the changing nature of masculinities*. London: Routledge.

Blazo, J.A., Carson, S., Czech, D.R. and Dees, W. (2014) A qualitative investigation of the sibling sport achievement experience. *The Sport Psychologist*, 28(1), 36–47.

Burke, P.J. and Stets, J.E. (2009) *Identity theory*. Oxford: Oxford University Press.

Claringbould, I. and Adriaanse, J. (2015) 'Silver cups versus ice creams': parental involvement with the construction of gender in the field of their son's soccer. *Sociology of Sport Journal*, 32(2), 201–219.

Coakley, J. (2006) The good father: parental expectations and youth sports. *Leisure Studies*, 25(2), 153–163.

Corbett, K. (2009) *Boyhoods: rethinking masculinities*. London: Yale University Press.

Dixon, M.A., Warner, S.M. and Bruening, J.E. (2008) More than just letting them play: parental influence on women's lifetime sport involvement. *Sociology of Sport Journal*, 25(4), 538–559.

FIFA (2019) *Women's football member associations survey report 2019*. Available from: https://img.fifa.com/image/upload/nq3ensohyxpuxov covj0.pdf [Accessed 8 July 2020].

Fredricks, J.A. and Eccles, J.S. (2005) Family socialization, gender, and sport motivation and involvement. *Sport Psychology*, 27(1), 3–31.

Gearson, K. (2010) Falling back on plan B: the children of the gender revolution face unchartered territory. In: Risman, B. (ed.) *Families as they really are*. London: W.W. Norton and Company, 378–392.

Gottzén, L. and Kremer-Sadlik, T. (2012) Fatherhood and youth sports: a balancing act between care and expectations. *Gender and Society*, 26(4), 639–664.

Greendorfer, S.L. and Lewko, J.H. (1978) Role of family members in sport socialization of children. *Research Quarterly American Alliance for Health, Physical Education and Recreation*, 49(2), 146–152.

Harrington, M. (2009) Sport mad, good dads: Australian fathering through leisure and sport practices. In: Kay, T. (ed.) *Fathering through sport and leisure*. Oxon: Routledge, 51–72.

Harwood, C. and Knight, C. (2009) Understanding parental stressors: an investigation of British tennis-parents. *Journal of Sports Sciences*, 27(4), 339–351.

Hatter, W., Vinter, L. and Williams, R. (2002) *Dads on dads: needs and expectations at home and at work*. Manchester: MORI Social Research Institute.

Haycock, D. and Smith, A. (2014) A family affair? Exploring the influence of childhood sport socialisation on young adults' leisure-sport careers in north-west England. *Leisure Studies*, 33(3), 285–304.

Hayes, S. (1996) *The cultural contradictions of motherhood*. New Haven: Yale University Press.

Hughes, C. (2002) *Key concepts in feminist theory and research*. London: Sage Publications.

Hughson, J. (2000) The boys are back in town: soccer and the social reproduction of masculinity. *Journal of Sport and Social Issues*, 24(1), 8–23.

Jeanes, R. and Magee, J. (2011) Come on my son! Examining fathers, masculinity and fathering through football. *Annals of Leisure Research*, 14(2–3), 273–288.

Kane, E.W. (2008) "No way my boys are going to be like that!" Parents' responses to children's gender nonconformity. In: Spade, J.Z. and Valentine, C.G. (eds.) *The kaleidoscope of gender: prisms, patterns, and possibilities*, 2nd edition. London: Sage Publications, 173–180.

Kay, T. (ed.) (2009) *Fathering through sport and leisure*. Oxon: Routledge.

Lopez, S. (1997) *Women on the ball: a guide to women's football*. London: Scarlet Press.

Lytton, H. and Romney, D.M. (1991) Parents' differential socialization of boys and girls: a meta-analysis. *Psychological Bulletin*, 109(2), 267–296.

McHale, S.H., Crouter, A.C. and Whiteman, S.D. (2003) The family contexts of gender development in childhood and adolescence. *Social Development*, 12(1), 125–148.

Messner, M.A. and Bozada-Deas, S. (2009) Separating the men from the moms: the making of adult gender segregation in youth sports. *Gender and Society*, 23(1), 49–71.

Raudsepp, L. and Viira, R. (2000) Influence of parents' and siblings' physical activity on activity levels of adolescents. *European Journal of Physical Education*, 5(2), 169–178.

Scraton, S., Fasting, K., Pfister, G. and Brunel, A. (1999) It's still a man's game? The experiences of top-level European women footballers. *International Review for the Sociology of Sport*, 34(2), 99–111.

Spowart, L., Hughson, J. and Shaw, S. (2008) Snowboarding mums carve out fresh tracks: resisting traditional motherhood discourse? *Annals of Leisure Research*, 11(1–2), 187–204.

Stirling, L. and Schulz, J. (2011) Women's football: still in the hands of men. *Sport Management International Journal*, 7(2), 53–78.

Stirrup, J., Duncombe, R. and Sandford, R. (2015) 'Intensive mothering' in the early years: the cultivation and consolidation of (physical) capital. *Sport, Education and Society*, 20(1), 89–106.

Stryker, S. (1980) *Symbolic interactionism: a social structural version*. London: The Benjamin/Cummings Publishing Company.

Such, L. (2009) Fatherhood, the morality of personal time and leisure-based parenting. In Kay, T. (ed.) *Fathering through sport and leisure*. Oxon: Routledge, 73–87.

Swanson, L. (2009) Complicating the 'soccer mom:' the cultural politics of forming class-based identity, distinction, and necessity. *Research Quarterly for Exercise and Sport*, 80(2), 345–354.

Thorne, B. (1993) *Gender play: girls and boys in school*. Buckingham: Open University Press.

Trussell, D.E. and Shaw, S.M. (2012) Organized youth sport and parenting in public and private spaces. *Leisure Sciences*, 34(5), 377–394.

UEFA (2015) *Women's football across the national associations 2014–15*. Available from: http://www.uefa.com/MultimediaFiles/Download/Women/General/02/03/27/84/2032784_DOWNLOAD.pdf [Accessed 27 December 2015].

UEFA (2017) *Women's football across the national associations 2017*. Available from: https://www.uefa.com/MultimediaFiles/Download/OfficialDocument/uefaorg/Women'sfootball/02/51/60/57/2516057_DOWNLOAD.pdf [Accessed 11 June 2019].

Valentine, G. (1997) 'My son's a bit dizzy', 'my wife's a bit soft': gender, children and cultures of parenting. *Gender, Place and Culture*, 4(1), 37–62.

Wedgwood, N. (2004) Kicking like a boy: schoolgirl Australian Rules Football and bi-gendered female embodiment. *Sociology of Sport Journal*, 21(2), 140–162.

West, C. and Zimmerman, D.H. (1987) Doing gender. *Gender and Society*, 1(2), 125–151.

Willms, N. (2009) Fathers and daughters: negotiating gendered relationships in sport. In: Kay, T. (ed.) *Fathering through sport and leisure*. Oxon: Routledge, 124–144.

8 Gender justice and social change
Beyond the football self

Those dreaded words floated across to me in the changing rooms: 'Will you run the line, Hanya?' I often thought that there was nothing worse than being a sub until it became layered with officiating duties. There was a paid referee sorted but often willing volunteers would have to run the line. I know my manager didn't want to ask me; almost embarrassed that she needed to. I remember making an offside call and being jeered at by the opposition team's supporters and I thought, 'I can't be bothered with this anymore'. Not too long after I was expecting my first child which made the decision to retire even easier. I had played football for over 20 years of my life, but I was ready to have my weekends back (to change nappies and breastfeed instead!).

My football self lives on even after retirement, like so many of the players in my research; it is not something that disappears when you stop playing. My football beginnings as described in Chapter 1 are concluded here but my love of football continues. An interest in football is a useful asset to have; it helps with silences when queuing at the photocopier at work, it provides a focus when speaking to undergraduates on a Monday morning, and above all else it gives me a sporting history. It's a little bit like an education: once you gain one, no one can ever take it away from you. Previous football experience affords you entry into an invisible club, a club you will always be part of, a club that gives you a long-lasting identity.

This is the reason why so many footballers reportedly struggle with retirement and injury; some go on to suffer with their mental health (Ramelea et al., 2017; Sanders and Stevinson, 2017) and with identity issues (Roderick, 2014; Pielichaty, 2019). This is possibly due to still *feeling* like a footballer, but this time you are not 'performing' footballer or 'doing' football. Identity loss can be likened to Goffman's (1959) dramaturgical approach to identity and performance; for injured or retired footballers the identity is maintained but the performance has disappeared. It's like a disentanglement identity quandary. It could be assumed that the more salient the football self, the more difficult it is to break that connection to participation. Chapter 3 discussed the importance and resonance of the football self to those who play, and Chapters 5–7 explained how this was embedded within family identities and parent performances. This exacerbates the importance and complexity of football retirement even more; it is not only part of the players' lives but encompasses family communities as well. This final chapter will summarise the current position of women's football, and provide insight into contemporary environmental concerns impacting the game before ending with a strategy for the future of the sport.

Where are we at?

Women's football cannot compete with men's football for spectators, media coverage, commercial appeal and many other things. It is played differently. It is a different sport. But it is also the same sport...

'Adding' women, bit by bit, to the football world is believed to lead eventually to an equitable situation. But inclusion does not equal equity; the presence of women is not enough.

(Dunn and Welford, 2015, 92)

It is this ever-present 'contradiction' which the players discussed in this book grappled with on a daily basis. They were football players but not in the 'real' game of football; they developed ways to normalise their participation so not to detract from their enjoyment of the game. Sport remains deeply ingrained in contemporary culture, politicised and problematised by government departments and academics the like. This book has highlighted the way in which sport continues to occupy challenging and complex physical and ideological spaces because of the stereotypical perceptions still surrounding girls and women playing sports. Football in the UK still endures its seemingly inseparable links with male dominance and masculinity.

The dynamism, complexities and uncertainties involved in the elite women's game as illustrated in Chapter 2 demonstrate the on-going and fluctuating issues related to football and specifically women's football. Writing this book during the Covid-19 pandemic makes it very difficult to predict the future of the women's game, as highlighted by Clarkson et al. (2020). What I can do though is draw upon interest points and dominant themes developed from my empirical data to offer some guidance and hope for the future of women's football.

Our British society has not experienced turbulence, disturbance, terror and uncertainty like this in recent history; Covid-19 has enveloped all that we know and forced change. The legacy of which we are yet to see, but it feels like women's lives and women's sports will be profoundly impacted. The United Nations (UN, 2020) policy brief detailed the effect Covid-19 has on women:

> The pandemic is deepening pre-existing inequalities, exposing vulnerabilities in social, political and economic systems which are in turn amplifying the impacts of the pandemic.
>
> (UN, 2020, 2)

These pre-existing inequalities are discussed in connection with unpaid work (such as care responsibilities), gender-based violence, and health and economic insecurities. Covid-19 is thought to be 'a test of our human spirit' (UN, 2020, 2) as it wreaks havoc physically and mentally on all who experience it (directly or indirectly), and particularly those already in vulnerable positions:

> The COVID-19 pandemic poses devastating risks for women and girls in fragile and conflict-affected contexts. Disruptions to critical health, humanitarian and development programmes can have life and death consequences where health systems may already be overwhelmed or largely non-existent.
>
> (UN, 2020, 20)

The effects of Covid-19 are amplified by the a priori cultural and social constraints and limitations surrounding womanhood more generally. These are also mirrored in the sporting sphere because sport and society have always been inextricably linked as the CEO of Women in Sport, Stephanie Hilborne, explains:

> It is true that mid-crisis we can only guess at what will happen afterwards and we can over-estimate its impact, but we are

already seeing worrying patterns emerge and a potential sce-
nario were women's sport returns to being undervalued, under-
funded and invisible.

(Hilborne, 2020)

These 'worrying patterns' have been demonstrated by the post-
ponement of the Women's European Championship and the suspension of girls' (not boys') elite football academies (McElwee,
2020). FIFPro (2020) explains that it is those already in precari-
ous and marginalised positions that the pandemic will negatively
impact the most. Their report highlights the vulnerability of the
women's game:

Due to its less established professional leagues, low salaries,
narrower scope of opportunities, uneven sponsorship deals and
less corporate investment, the fragility of the women's football
eco-system is exposed by the current situation.

(FIFPro, 2020, 2)

The Covid-19 pandemic has revealed the insecure state of elite
women's football globally, and it is now time to change this. The
FIFPro report (2020, 7–8) provides a breakdown of industry actions needed to combat the recovery of women's elite football which
include financial and safety measures required to safeguard women
footballers. The pandemic has lifted the *societal cloak* which was
obscuring the details, issues and inequalities surrounding girls'
and women's football. The creation and visibility of professional
leagues and tournaments alongside increased participation numbers is not enough to represent equality. Institutional, interactional
and individual change (see Risman, 2004, 437) and firm business
models must provide the core to enact real, social change.

Praxis, policy and practice

It is important at this juncture to review the policy around girls'
and women's sport and also football to understand how this feeds
into a potential strategy for social transformation. For decades
girls' sport participation dropout rates have been higher than that
of boys: 'Only 8% of girls meet the Chief Medical Officer's rec-
ommendation that young people aged 5–18 should do 60 minutes
of physical activity every day' (Youth Sport Trust, 2017, 2). This
was mirrored by some of the players discussed within this book,

whereby the seemingly constant identities of those with salient football selves did alter when they began to question their future in the sport due to university, career choices and family aspirations. Providing a more robust support network for players who wish to continue their playing alongside their other lifestyle choices would be a useful pathway for players in the UK. University scholarships, courses on 'football careers and participation' and flexible clubs catering for U17s and older would assist in this progression. Extra assistance and support for players with salient football selves who are on the cusp of retirement would also be beneficial, as it is these players to whom football means so much who should be supported to continue in the game.

It is the Football Association (FA) to which we need to look for policy change, provision for retired footballers and also to change the stereotypical views around girls, women and football. The 2017–2020 strategy, *The Gameplan for Growth*, does acknowledge the social and cultural challenges within the game, stating a need to combat the stereotypical perceptions linked to the game by 'presenting the reality of women's and girls' football' (FA, 2017, 22) with an emphasis on the teamwork, enjoyment, fun, friendship and fitness aspects of the game. The FA also recognises:

> It's not just girls whom we need to appeal. Crucially, it's their parents, carers and teachers, many of whom may still operate by the stereotypes we need to dispel.
>
> (FA, 2017, 22)

The FA demonstrates an awareness of the challenges that the game still faces; these have been explored in some considerable depth in this book. Furthermore, the parents and family members in this study were all mindful of the stereotypical image that constrained opportunities in girls' and women's football. It is these passionate football parents who could be utilised by the FA to help to 'dispel' the stereotypes that others may still have of the game in relation to their future plans. *The Gameplan for Growth* has now ended, and the final report places green ticks next to all the FA's targets: doubling participation, doubling fan base and world stage success (FA, 2020a). The social and cultural perception of girls' and women's football, however, is not addressed in the final report, and it is this 'cultural hangover' from previous decades that continues to plague the game.

The FA's 2020–2024 strategy for women and girls, *Inspiring Positive Change*, outlines another eight priorities, none of which directly report on the socio-cultural barriers that impact upon participation. The focus areas of the strategy are on school opportunities, clear player pathways, sport for all and a new management board for the elite game. These are all very welcomed and needed but it is concerning that the underlying, cultural position of girls' and women's football is not addressed. Regarding coaching, the strategy does seek to 'normalise women in football coaching, but also to provide aspirational, relatable and credible female role models for future generations' (FA, 2020b, 39). This connection to normalising is significant and the FA also realises that 'removing barriers and making football more relevant to young girls' lives is essential' (FA, 2020b, 17). Although, the removal of barriers, here in connection with teenage participation, is linked to the girls themselves regarding player self-esteem (FA, 2020b, 18) rather than addressing the wider socio-cultural picture. This type of intervention can be related to 'fix the women' campaigns (see Shaw and Frisby, 2006), whereby liberal feminist approaches to gender equity focus on women being the 'problem'. Thereby, targeting players to work on their own self-esteem in connection with participation ignores the wider-social issues around stereotyping which can contribute to this low self-esteem in the first instance. It is problematic to build a new strategy upon the unstable socio-cultural platform that we are balancing on. The FA's umbrella strategy, *Time for Change*, however, does look to directly address inequalities in football (FA, 2020c) and presents a significantly uplifting vision for the sport.

Other sports organisations have prioritised their efforts to bring family to the fore, as demonstrated in the empirical data presented in this book. It is cardinal that sports organisations place reasonable value on the role of families in sport as a means to encourage and develop the access and participation for girls and women. Sport England's 2016–2021 strategy, *Towards an Active Nation*, presents a detailed way to tackle inactivity and boost impact, and their Families Fund was designated specifically for projects seeking to combine family life and sport to provide long-lasting benefits (Sport England, 2016).

The Daughters and Dads Active and Empowered (DADEE) programme developed in 2014 by the University of Newcastle, Australia, targets dads 'as the agents of change' to improve their daughter's relationship with physical activity. This programme has been very successful in engaging over 600 daughters and 500 dads since 2015 (DADEE, 2020). In 2018 this programme came to the UK after Women in Sport in partnership with the Fatherhood Institute, Fulham Football club and the English Football League Trust received Sport England Lottery Funding to create a project aimed at low-income families in London (Women in Sport, 2018). Sport England (2020) have also pledged £1 million towards the development and legacy of women's football in connection with the UEFA European Championship in 2022 to be hosted by England. The plan is to 'create recreational women's football opportunities' which will be situated across the proposed host locations of London, Trafford, Manchester, Sheffield, Rotherham, Wigan and Leigh, Brighton and Hove, Southampton and Milton Keynes.

There is certainly investment going into girls' and women's football around this time and with the excitement of an international tournament on the horizon bodes well for the future of the game. The FA's new strategy for girls and women, despite downplaying societal issues, does still provide an exciting opportunity for growth and access to participation across all pathways and levels. For change to be impactful beyond the surface level, investment and resources must transcend the mere economics of the game and reach to the depths of social and cultural change. The following section will highlight a potential way to confront this utilising a strategy for gender justice for girls' and women's football which I have developed for this book.

A strategy for gender justice

There are opportunities presented in this book and in the face of global turbulence to renew and create a more sustainable game for girls and women to play. Gender justice is a useful lens in which to understand this further and I have utilised my own work in connection with higher education (see Pielichaty 2021) to frame this section. Gender justice has also been linked to sport and leisure vis-à-vis social, economic and political (in)equalities (see Watson and Scraton, 2017). As presented by Watson and Scraton (2017) gender justice can be utilised to transform sport if resources and support systems are in place. The *distribution* and *recognition* prongs to gender, regarding class/labour and status, respectively, must be understood for gender justice to be effective (Fraser, 2007). For example, the way in which elite women's football is politically positioned and economically rewarded must also be informed by its cultural standing. Gender justice, for Watson and Scraton (2017), is not just a *feminist issue* but a humanitarian one, and sites for gender justice can be taken from everyday occasions:

The material contexts of leisure and sport, be that time, access, resources or the cultural 'circuits' in which female subjects 'perform' their daily lives, require continued engagement and analysis.

(Watson and Scraton, 2017, 52)

British football is a space and site for inequalities, and we need to challenge 'gender injustices that persistently marginalise' (Watson and Scraton, 2017, 44–45) such as those faced in girls' and women's football. To do this I have created a strategy for gender justice developed specifically for this book. This strategy is an academic model to catalyse social change and should sit alongside other organisational goals in a team effort for gender justice.

I have created this strategy based on my own five facets of gender justice in connection with higher education (Pielichaty, 2021) and advance it here to incorporate my own knowledge of girls' and women's football. It is important that I outline my five facets of gender justice as originally utilised and then go on to explain how these will be transferred to the world of sport. The facets are reflection, university ethos, communities, curriculum and language (Pielichaty, 2021, 5–6). First, *reflection* relates to a continuous period of reflexivity and awareness, looking both back and forwards to understand how equalities and inclusivities are presented internally and externally. For gender justice to be transformational then self-reflection must be taken seriously and threaded through the entire process and organisation. Second, *ethos* refers to the philosophy of an organisation and what messages are being conveyed through its being. Third, *communities* be that all the constituent parts that come together to socially and culturally shape an organisation must buy-in to a shared vision of equality and change. Fourth, *curriculum* is the principles of teaching and learning which must be grounded in a pedagogy that empowers and is formed based on equality and freedom. Finally, the *language* that is used and conveyed should seek to challenge stereotypes and address formal and informal narrative discrepancies that can undermine activism. In application to girls' and women's football, the facet of 'curriculum' will be regarded as 'education' to mean both coach education and player training. The following table presents my strategy for gender justice in connection with girls' and women's football (Table 8.1).

This strategy presents gender justice as relational to *visibility* and the need to ensure girls and women footballers and those working in and around the sport are seen, heard and accepted. Visibility is

Table 8.1 A Strategy for Gender Justice in Girls' and Women's Football (Based upon Pielichaty's (2021) Five Facets of Gender Justice).

Facets of Gender Justice	*Actions for Activism*

Reflection	• Each footballing community must take time to reflect on how their community currently feeds in to the football gender imbalance;
	• Reflection is a process which should be continuous and mobile to align to advancements and challenges;
	• Reflections should be made across several areas, including:
	  o Ethos – community values, vision and culture;
	  o Communities – current interest groups, members, an understanding of the communication trail between groups;
	  o Education – pedagogy, design, content, suitability of spaces for inclusion and equality to foster, commitment to values;
	  o Language – assessment of key message and how they are conveyed, marketing materials, website design, use of images, media content, press coverage, social cues, conversations, avenues to 'speak out'.

Ethos	• The ethos and culture of football communities to be:
	  o Underpinned by equality and gender justice;
	  o Committed to a shared vision of equality;
	  o Intolerant of intolerance;
	  o Dedicated to bringing about social change for girls' and women's football and footballers.

(Continued)

Facets of Gender Justice	Actions for Activism
Communities	• All community members to be individual pioneers and advocates for girls' and women's football across all contexts and places;
	• The football self is varied, and many versions of selves must be included into football communities;
	• **Player communities** to:
	o Continue to play and enjoy football;
	o Acknowledge and accept that 'any type' of girl may want to play football;
	o Challenge barriers to playing sport;
	o Not accept gender-based stereotyping or discrimination, speak out and act.
	• **Family communities** to provide time and access opportunities for their family member (mother, daughter, sister);
	• **Social communities** (families, friends, colleagues) to have the opportunity to talk and learn about women's football;
	• **Policy communities** must place value on the progress of girls' and women's football through investment and funding support. Policy and political advocating should be linked to equality and justice.
	• **Clubs and governing communities** to:
	o Provide women with opportunities to play, manage, lead and watch football on a global stage;
	o Invest in all levels of the game to ensure provision is world-leading, appropriate, safe and empowering;
	o Provide initiatives to allow players, managers, coaches and spectators to speak out and be transparent about gender-based stereotyping or discrimination;
	o Address socio-cultural challenges more deeply within strategy and policy.
	• **Broadcasters and media communities** to:
	o Ensure punditry panels, media coverage and reporting of football to be equal, fair and gender balanced;
	o Media and press coverage to be informed, accurate, empowering and visible.
	• **Businesses communities** to sponsor, invest and buy-into women's football.

Education	• Coach education to be embedded by feminist pedagogy and an understanding of inclusivity and acceptance; • Training and education to be provided in clubs and schools around gender equality and inclusivity; • Design and implement social interaction spaces to offer opportunities to watch and play football; • Use technical examples from women's football during training and football educational courses.
Language	• Girls' and women's voices must be heard and discourses surrounding football need to be actively managed; • Words and stories matter; transformation will come from positive and empowering narrative; • The narrative of football should be equal, for example tournaments to be labelled appropriately, not simply the *World Cup* and then the *Women's World Cup*; • Individuals and communities to take personal responsibility for how they learn about, discuss and relay information; • Language across platforms and resources to be empowering, equal and responsible.

powerful; it helps to create normative assumptions and expectations about the world we live in. Visibility is a political matter because gender politics is often about the constraint and marginalisation of voice and presence. We must be able to see girls and women playing, managing and officiating football in order to understand it is an accepted, valid and 'normal' part of society. This strategy for gender justice is the first iteration of its kind and therefore provides a stepping stone towards further research and inquiry. Gender justice is dynamic and mobile and will need constantly addressing in connection with socio-cultural progress and change.

Change and growth

The strategy presented in the previous section values women and girls and their engagement with football. There are already signs that the future of women's football is one worth watching. For example, the Los Angeles team, *Angel City*, is due to enter the NWSL in 2022 which is empowering due to its female-dominated management board (NWSL, 2020). This move which has celebrity backing offers a distinctly new offering to the current business model and will be eagerly observed by other leagues globally. Acts of activism are happening on the global stage, and my empirical data also show how everyday activisms can be significant in contributing to social change.

There are a lot of positives to report on currently in girls' and women's sport and football more specifically. As Chapter 2 highlighted, the appetite for the women's elite game appears strong and the international competitions have taken the sport to new heights. The participation numbers are healthy and growing; women and girls have access to football across many platforms and with support of family and friends. The game is full of potential, passion and drive and undoubtedly progress is being made. My empirical data have demonstrated that girls' and women's football continues to face barriers based on archaic views of gender hierarchies (see Chapter 4), but despite this there are some positive developments: signs of cultural change. For example, young girls inspired friends and families to get involved in football, and players and their family members carved out new ways in which to manage and create opportunities for participation. My research sites were positive hubs for girls' and women's engagement with football, but it is also the spaces in-between and away from these hubs that 'social work' needs to be done.

I cannot help but feel there is still much more to do. It is the core and depths of the game that have yet to be addressed in full.

The deep-seated hegemonic roots of the sport continue to hamper the growth of girls' and women's football. Its social perception and cultural positioning sustains a weak position at the foundation level of the sport. If this is not fully addressed, participation numbers may continue to increase alongside tournament success but its poor cultural status will stay untouched. If, however, the strategy for gender justice is embedded across the footballing communities then social change can be realised.

Future areas for academic exploration

Research into girls' and women's football is at an important juncture within academia. The increased development and attention on the sport means that it presents many opportunities for further study and research. My study is one of the first to explore the lives of girls and women footballers in connection with their family. It is hoped that this publication will spark an interest in this topic as there is still so much more to explore. Some general areas for further inquiry are listed here:

- Further examination of parental relationships with girls and women footballers, especially mothers;
- A closer investigation into family structures in relation to football support and provision;
- A comparative study between boys' and girls' football experiences in relation to gender identity and family relationships;
- An investigation of the match-day experiences of girls and women players in connection with gender and family;
- Extended exploration into the role of beauty and appearance in the elite women's game;
- Deeper investigation into the role and relationships between siblings and grandparents and footballers;
- An examination of everyday activisms and gender justice within girls' and women's football across other sites;
- A global comparative study between experiences of girls and women footballers in the UK in relation to players in other countries with regard to family relationships and football identities.

Conclusion

Sometimes it is difficult to comprehend how complex and contested the game of football is for the girls and women who play it. How can 22 individuals kicking a ball around contribute to so much inequality, angst and struggle? But as I have explained in this book, the football self is much more than the sum of football's component parts. It is not about the grass, the ball, the goal, the kit, the teammates, the clubhouse, the bandstand…. it is about everything together and so much more as well. We all care about football, and we care so deeply that it causes division, inequality, injustice and hurt; but it can also be the source of hope, change, freedom and light. This book has highlighted the passion, love and determination girls and women have in order to achieve in football. A masculine ethos continues to dominate the sport in England but many girls and women players, along with their parents, siblings, grandparents and coaches are working hard to challenge this and are making a difference.

References

Clarkson, B.G., Culvin, A. Pope S. and Parry, K.D. (2020) Covid-19: reflections on threat and uncertainty for the future of elite women's football in England. *Managing Sport and Leisure*, doi:10.1080/23750472.202 0.1766377.

DADEE (2020) *History*. Available from: https://www.daughtersanddads. com.au/about/history/ [Accessed 22 July 2020].

Dunn, C. and Welford, J. (2015) *Football and the FA women's super league: structure, governance and impact*. London: Palgrave.

FA (2017) *The gameplan for growth: the FA's strategy for women's and girls' football: 2017–2020*. Available from: file:///C:/Users/PC/Downloads/ fawomensstrategydocfinal-13317%20(1).pdf [Accessed 11 June 2019].

FA (2020a) *The gameplan for growth the FA's strategy for women's and girls' football: 2017–2020 final review and report*. Available from: file:/// C:/Users/PC/Downloads/the-gameplan-for-growth-final-review-and- report.pdf [Accessed 23 July 2020].

FA (2020b) *Inspiring positive change: the FA's strategy for women's and girls' football: 2020–2024*. Available from: https://www.thefa.com/news/2020/ oct/19/new-fa-womens-strategy-launched-191020 [Accessed 20 January 2021].

FA (2020c) *Time for change: the FA strategy 2020–2024*. Available from: https://www.thefa.com/about-football-association/what-we-do/ strategy#group-section-OUR-STRATEGY-iRH4tpTunF [Accessed 12 January 2021].

FIFPro (2020) *COVID-19: implications for professional women's football*. Available from: https://www.fifpro.org/media/mybpsvym/fifpro- womens-football-covid19.pdf [Accessed 23 July 2020].

Fraser, N. (2007) Feminist politics in the age of recognition: a two-dimensional approach to gender justice. *Studies in Social Justice*, 1(1), 23–35.

Goffman, E. (1959) *The presentation of the self in everyday life*. London: Penguin Books.

Hilborne, S. (2020) What will Covid-19 mean for the future of women's sport? Available from: https://www.womeninsport.org/opinion/covid-19-future-of-womens-sport/ [Accessed 16 July 2020].

McElwee, M. (2020) Youth football embroiled in equality row as elite girls told to stop playing while male academies continue. *The Telegraph*, 5 November. Available from: https://www.telegraph.co.uk/football/2020/11/05/youth-football-embroiled-equality-row-elite-girls-told-stop/ [Accessed 11 November 2020].

NWSL (2020) *National Women's Soccer League awards expansion team rights to Los Angeles*. Available from: https://www.nwslsoccer.com/news/article/national-womens-soccer-league-awards-expansion-team-rights-to-los-angeles [Accessed 22 July 2020].

Pielichaty, H. (2019) Identity salience and the football self: a critical ethnographic study of women and girls in football. *Qualitative Research in Sport, Exercise and Health*, 11(4), 527–542.

Pielichaty, H. (2021) Embedding gender justice in higher education: an example from sports business management. *IMPact*, 4(1), 1–8.

Ramelea, S.V., Aokib, H., Kerkhoffs, G.M.M.J. and Gouttebarge, V. (2017) Mental health in retired professional football players: 12-month incidence, adverse life events and support. *Psychology of Sport and Exercise*, 28, 85–90.

Risman, B.J. (2004) Gender as a social structure: theory wrestling with activism. *Gender and Society*, 18(4), 429–450.

Roderick, M. (2014) From identification to dis-identification: case studies of job loss in professional football. *Qualitative Research in Sport, Exercise and Health*, 6(2), 143–160.

Sanders, G. and Stevinson, C. (2017) Associations between retirement reasons, chronic pain, athletic identity, and depressive symptoms among former professional footballers. *European Journal of Sport Science*, 17(10), 1311–1318.

Shaw, S. and Frisby, W. (2006) Can gender equity be more equitable? Promoting an alternative frame for sport management research, education, and practice. *Journal of Sport Management*, 20(4), 483–509.

Sport England (2016) *Sport England: towards an active nation strategy 2016–2021*. Available from: https://sportengland-production-files.s3.eu-west-2.amazonaws.com/s3fs-public/sport-england-towards-an-active-nation.pdf?zE6hDbFaa9dNK8tRqxP2HuVIM2Ls79HG [Accessed 22 July 2020].

Sport England (2020) *Women's football given £1m boost*. Available from: https://www.sportengland.org/news/womens-football-given-1m-boost [Accessed 24 July 2020].

United Nations (2020) Policy brief: the impact of COVID-19 on women. *United Nations*, 9 April. Available from: https://www.un.org/sexualviolenceinconflict/wp-content/uploads/2020/06/

report/policy-brief-the-impact-of-covid-19-on-women/policy-brief-the-impact-of-covid-19-on-women-en-1.pdf [Accessed 16 July 2020].

Watson, B. and Scraton, S. (2017) Gender justice and leisure sport feminisms. In Long, J., Fletcher, T. and Watson, B. (eds.) *Sport, leisure and social justice*. London: Routledge, 43–57.

Women in Sport (2018) *Women in Sport in partnership with the Fatherhood Institute, Fulham Football Club and the EFL Trust wins National Lottery funding from Sport England to help dads and daughters get active together*. Available from: https://www.womeninsport.org/press-release/women-in-sport-in-partnership-with-the-fatherhood-institute-fulham-football-club-and-the-efl-trust-wins-national-lottery-funding-from-sport-england-to-help-dads-and-daughters-get-active-together/ [Accessed 22 July 2020].

Youth Sport Trust (2017) *Key findings from girls active survey November 2017*. Available from: https://www.womeninsport.org/wp-content/uploads/2017/11/Girls-Active-statistics-1.pdf [Accessed 23 July 2020].

Index

Note: **Bold** page numbers refer to tables and *italic* page numbers refer to figures.